ARCHITECTURE

AT

AHMEDABAD,

THE CAPITAL OF GOOZERAT

PHOTOGRAPHED BY COLONEL BIGGS R. A.

ARCHITECTURE

AT

AHMEDABAD,

THE CAPITAL OF GOOZERAT

PHOTOGRAPHED BY COLONEL BIGGS R. A.

WITH AN HISTORICAL AND DESCRIPTIVE SKETCH

BY THEODORE C. HOPE

AND

ARCHITECTURAL NOTES

BY JAMES FERGUSSON

GYAN

Published by

Gyan Publishing House
5, Ansari Road
Daryaganj, New Delhi-110002
Phone: 011-47034999, 9811692060
E-mail: books@gyanbooks.com

Distribution Network
gyanbooks.com
India, USA, Canada, UK, Australia

ISBN: 978-93-6433-346-7 (PB)
First Published, 1866

2nd Impression 2024

Printed at: Gyan Press, Delhi.

ARCHITECTURE AT AHMEDABAD, THE CAPITAL OF GOOZERAT PHOTOGRAPHED BY COLONEL BIGGS R. A.

Author: THEODORE C. HOPE, JAMES FERGUSSON

THE SACRED HILL OF SHUTROONJYE.

ARCHITECTURE

AT

AHMEDABAD,

THE CAPITAL OF GOOZERAT,

PHOTOGRAPHED BY COLONEL BIGGS, R.A.

WITH AN HISTORICAL AND DESCRIPTIVE SKETCH,

BY THEODORE C. HOPE,

BOMBAY CIVIL SERVICE,

AND

ARCHITECTURAL NOTES

BY JAMES FERGUSSON, F.R.S., M.R.A.S.,

FELLOW ROYAL INST. BRIT. ARCHITECTS.

PUBLISHED FOR THE COMMITTEE OF ARCHITECTURAL ANTIQUITIES OF WESTERN INDIA,
UNDER THE PATRONAGE OF

PREMCHUND RAICHUND.

LONDON:

JOHN MURRAY, ALBEMARLE STREET.

1866.

To the Memory

OF

THE HON^BLE ALEXANDER KINLOCH FORBES,

LATE OF THE BOMBAY CIVIL SERVICE, AND PUISNE JUDGE OF THE HIGH COURT OF BOMBAY,

AUTHOR OF THE "RÁS MÁLÁ," ETC.,

THIS WORK,

IN WHICH HE TOOK A SPECIAL INTEREST,

IS AFFECTIONATELY AND MOURNFULLY INSCRIBED

BY SOME

IN WHOM HIS GENIUS FIRST AWAKENED A LOVE

FOR THE ROMANTIC HISTORY AND GRACEFUL ARCHITECTURE

OF GOOZERAT.

PREFACE.

THE Government of Bombay has at various times taken steps towards portraying and presenting to the public portions of the magnificent architecture with which the Presidency and the territories bordering on it abound. About ten years ago, Captain (now Colonel) Biggs and Dr. Pigou were employed to take photographs at Beejapoor, and in Dharwar and Mysore. Subsequently a series of plans and drawings of Beejapoor, which had been prepared under the superintendence of Captain Hart, were published for the Government under the editorship of Mr. James Fergusson; and more recently still, Colonel Biggs took for the same authority a number of photographs of Ahmedabad. In February 1865 the undermentioned gentlemen were requested by his Excellency, Sir H. Bartle E. Frere, K.S.I., K.C.B., Governor of Bombay, to form themselves into a committee, with the view of publishing the materials collected as above described, and others to be procured, in the form of a comprehensive series of volumes on the Architectural Antiquities of Western India.

The Hon. W. E. FRERE.
The Hon. A. K. FORBES.
The Hon. H. NEWTON.
The Hon. W. R. CASSELS.
Sir JAMSETJEE JEEJEEBHOY, Bart.
The Hon. RUSTOMJEE J. JEEJEEBHOY.
The Hon. PREMABHAI HEMABHAI.
The Hon. JUGONATH SUNKERSETT.
Rev. Dr. WILSON.
T. C. HAYLLAR, Esq.
Sir A. GRANT, Bart.
W. WORDSWORTH, Esq.
BHAU DAJEE, Esq.
J. TRUBSHAWE, Esq.
E. I. HOWARD, Esq.

*

The expense of producing illustrated works of the description contemplated being necessarily so heavy that, even if sold at cost price they would be within the reach of a comparatively small portion of the public, certain native gentlemen volunteered, for the honour of their country and the greater diffusion of an acquaintance with it, each to take one volume under his patronage and contribute £1000 towards its publication. Mr. Premchund Raichund, a Jain and a native of Goozerat, has very liberally taken under his patronage two volumes, of which this is one, and the other, containing some of the principal edifices in Dharwar and Mysore, will appear shortly. A third volume, containing architecture at Beejapoor, an old Mahometan capital in the Deccan, will appear simultaneously with this, under the patronage of Mr. Kursondas Madhowdas. The three works have been produced under the gratuitous editorship and superintendence of Mr. T. C. Hope, of the Bombay Civil Service, who has likewise presented the historical and descriptive sketch contained in this volume. It is hoped that they may ultimately be followed by three more: the first embracing the early Hindoo and Jaina architecture of Goozerat; the second, the Cave-Temples of Western India; and the third, the old cities of Wurungol, Kuleán, Golconda, Goolburga, etc., together with the Hill Forts of the Deccan, and other miscellaneous objects of interest.

CONTENTS.

b

LIST OF ILLUSTRATIONS.

PHOTOGRAPHS:—

PHOTOGRAPHS—*continued.*

PHOTOGRAPHS—*continued.*

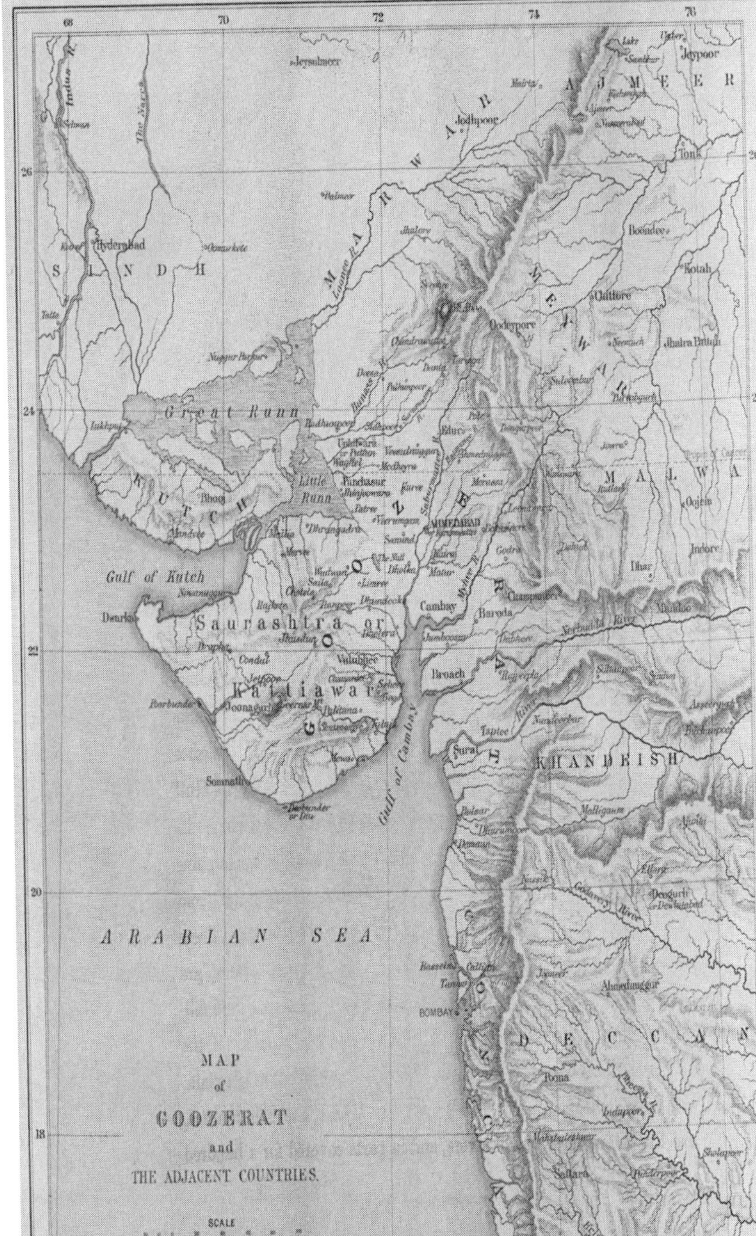

London: John Murray, Albemarle S[t]

PART I.

HISTORICAL SKETCH.

AHMEDABAD is believed to have been founded in the eleventh century, and has for the last four hundred and fifty years been the capital of Goozerat. In size and importance it now ranks next to Bombay among the cities of Western India. Goozerat, according to the permanent boundaries indicated by natural formation and the language of the people, is about equal to Great Britain in extent, and somewhat resembles a horse-shoe in shape. The Gulf of Cambay forms its inner boundary, and expands into the Arabian Sea, which washes it on the south-west, and turning northward, is merged in the Gulf of Kutch and the desert, often inundated Runn, which cover its whole western side. To the north-east, long ranges of mountains broken only by the debouchures of mighty rivers, cut it off from Marwar, Meywár, Málwa, Khandeish, and the rest of India. These mountains, rugged, bold, and throwing out frequent spurs, are covered with forests rich in the romantic beauty of stream and fell, where gigantic creepers scale in wild luxuriance the summits of the tallest trees. Gradually they subside into a broad alluvial plain, irrigated by the Nerbudda, the Taptee, the Myhee, the Sáburmuttee, the Bunás, and many minor rivers, and in parts covered for a hundred miles on end with groves of trees, like those of an English park. The south-western peninsula, formerly called Sauráshtra, or Soreth, and now Kattiawar, is for the most part gracefully undulating, with a fringe of hills along the coast, and abounds in good water and pasturage. Here and there lofty peaks, Chámárdee, Sehore, Shutroonjye, and Geernár, tower suddenly out of the level plain as if in rivalry of Áboo and Champaneer, the great bastions of the north-eastern range—all alike remarkable in that religion has for ages hovered around their summits, while dynasties arose and passed away at their feet—Chámárdee, beside which a capital of Goozerat was overwhelmed with sudden and mysterious ruin; Sehore, whose battered towers still guard the City of the Lion; Shutroonjye, sacred from all time, restored after barbarian ravages whilst our Saxon forefathers were landing on the British coast, and covered by many hundred well-served fanes; Geernár, the six-peaked mount of Jain and Hindoo faith and protector of the Lunar race; Champaneer, whose red-eyed goddess dealt ruin upon those who loved her well; Áboo, most favoured by the nymphs of lake and grove, out of whose fire-fountain, at the saintly Vashishta's prayer, arose the great progenitors of the Rajpoot race, and went forth to subdue the world to purity and faith and love. Equal in fame to these, but on the sea-coast, stand Puttun Somnáth, the temple of the "Lord of the Moon," Shiva, the Sun, or Baal, the patron of dark rites and deeds, whose oracles were a power in India which the whole strength of the Moslem invader was strained to crush; and Dwarka, where reigned, and now is worshipped, the "heaven-born Krishna, the graceful lover of Radhá." The coasts of Goozerat form a considerable portion of what was known of India to the ancients. They possess numerous harbours, among which may be mentioned Broach, the Barygaza of Ptolemy and Arrian, where still stands the tree which is thought to have suggested to Milton his description of the shelter of our first parents; Bulsar and Peerum, whose pirates used to engage the fleets of the neighbouring states; Surat and Cambay, early seats of British settlement and trade; Mowa, Gopnáth, Gundévee, &c. Through these ports was carried on till recently much of the trade of Upper India, in addition to that of Goozerat itself, comprising cotton, indigo, tobacco, opium, grain of all sorts, paper, cloth, agates, cornelians, horses, &c. The population consists of several distinct elements, each holding its appropriate position in the whole, and resembling each other in little more than that all are bold and warlike. The aboriginal Bheels and Koolies, swarthy children of the bow, still lord it in the forest and on the mountain; but elsewhere they have either blended with, or been displaced by, successive waves of immigration, among which the fair-haired Káthi still proclaims his Scythic origin, and the chivalrous Rajpoot maintains his political supremacy.

Possessing, as we have seen, a central and naturally defended position, an extensive seaboard, a fertile soil, and a high-spirited people, Goozerat has from the earliest times had a distinct and self-asserting nationality, a position in history disproportioned to its area, and a vitality which has ever surmounted foreign conquest and internal strife, and triumphs even now, when its cotton rules the Liverpool market and its merchants are among the most enlightened and wealthy in India. In war, the Rajpoot clanship was a material element of strength; and in peace, the liberality and devotion of Rajpoot princes so developed the national taste for letters and art that fresh traces of the former are ever rewarding patient research, while the latter, after leading captive even the Moslem conqueror, is still alive and vigorous, ranging modern beside ancient triumphs in their common seat. To bring forward such events and traits as are calculated to suggest how high standards of honour, faith, and art harmonized, and acted and reacted upon each other in the national life, will be a principal endeavour in the following historical sketch.

Of the early inhabitants of this, as of other parts of India, no authentic accounts exist; but many of the principal seats of power are believed to have been originally in their hands, and conquered from them, not founded, by the tribes which at various periods invaded India from the north, and subjugated, though they could not extirpate them. That those of Goozerat were numerous and strong is beyond doubt, for their city (the present Dholka) and their foreign conquests are mentioned in the great Hindoo epic, the Maháhhárata, and as late as the eleventh century one of their Chiefs is said to have brought a hundred thousand men into the field not far from where Ahmedabad now stands. The conquerors were, however, established in Sauráshtra and on the opposite coast long before the Christian era, and may be traced in the traditional history of the Yádoo race, in rock inscriptions and ancient shrines or cities, and in the commerce which they maintained with Egypt and Arabia. Next in order come the Bactrian kings, Demetrius and Menander, who made conquests in India in the second century before our era, and the last of whom, at least, must have been influential, if not paramount, in Goozerat, since his coins were still current in the first century after Christ. About the Christian era a dynasty rose to power, of which we have somewhat more reliable accounts, and which lasted till about A.D. 250. They were styled Sinhas, or Sáhs, and are believed to have been of Parthian origin,* and to have worshipped the sun. Sehore, the Lion City, was their capital; but their sway extended far south to Sattára and Kolapoor, so as to comprehend most of the modern Presidency of Bombay. They are also thought to have subdued the island of Lanká, and given it the name of Sinhaladwipa (whence Ceylon), and to have carried their arms far into the Eastern Archipelago. About the middle of the third century the Sáhs were superseded by the Guptas, who appear to have invaded Goozerat after gradually subduing the Indo-Scythian dynasty of central and northern India. Their rule must, however, have been of but brief duration, for coins of only two of their monarchs are forthcoming, and in A.D. 319 arose a new line of native origin, whose capital was Vulubhee, at the foot of the hills of Chámárdee.

The kingdom of Vulubhee lasted till about the middle of the seventh century, when it was overwhelmed by barbarian invaders of Sassanian origin. Its authority appears to have been complete throughout Goozerat and Kutch, but traces are not wanting of a far wider rule. The extent and magnificence of the capital are attested by Chinese travellers and by the ruins still in existence. Its monarchs were for the most part of the Brahminical faith, and assiduous worshippers of Shiva; but in the fifth century one of them, Shiláditya, was converted to the Jaina sect, after a public disputation of the champions of the rival creeds, similar to those of early and mediæval Christianity.

The Jains, who here take an early place in Goozerat history, may be briefly described as a most ancient sect analogous to the Budd-

* A list of nineteen monarchs of this race has recently been deduced by the Hon. Mr. Justice Newton from their coins, on which the sun is a conspicuous emblem.

hists, whose chief peculiarities are a tenderness for animal life, and the substitution of twenty-four Teerthunkers, or saints, who have attained final reunion with the Divine Spirit, for Sákya Mooni, whom alone the Buddhists recognise as their mortal teacher. Mahávira, the last of the Teerthunkers, was nearly contemporary with Sákya, and died about 600 B.C., from which period the Buddhist religion dates its rise. After some centuries of expansion and triumph, Buddhists of all denominations had to endure long and sanguinary persecution from the Brahminical supporters of the religion of the Vedas, by which the adherents of Sákya, though spreading their tenets to Thibet and the far East, were gradually exterminated in India, and by the twelfth century had ceased to exist there. Not so the Jains, who maintained their ground, principally in Goozerat and Mysore, and still survive to hold in their hands a large proportion of the wealth and trade of India. They were remarkable for the costliness and beauty of their temples. Mysore and Dharwar still abound in them, but the most ancient are to be found at Geernár, the most exquisite on Mount Áboo, and the most extensive and still flourishing at Shutroonjye, near Palitána.* These last were restored and beautified by Shiláditya, the royal convert of the Vulubhee race to whom we have already alluded, and at the present day do ample justice to the following description from the graceful pen of the author of the Rás Málá:—"Shutroonjye is one of the most ancient and most sacred shrines of the Jain religion. It is described as the first of places of pilgrimage, the bridal hall of those who would marry everlasting rest; like our own sacred Iona, it is not destined to be destroyed, even at the end of the world." "There is hardly a city in India, throughout its length

* *See* Frontispiece.

and breadth, from the river of Sindh to the sacred Ganges, from Heemâla's diadem of ice peaks, to the throne of his virgin daughter, Roodra's destined bride, that has not supplied, at one time or another, contributions of wealth to the edifices which crown the hill of Pâleetâna; street after street, and square after square, extend these shrines of the Jain faith, with their stately enclosures, half palace, half fortress, raised, in marble magnificence, upon the lonely and majestic mountain, and like the mansions of another world, far removed in upper air from the ordinary tread of mortals. In the dark recess of each temple one image or more of Adeenâth, of Ujeet, or of some other of the Teerthunkers, is seated, whose alabaster features, wearing an expression of listless repose, are rendered dimly visible by the faint light shed from silver lamps; incense perfumes the air, and bare-footed, with noiseless tread upon the polished floors, the female votaries, glittering in scarlet and gold, move round and round in circles, chanting forth their monotonous, but not unmelodious hymns." *

After the fall of Vulubhee succeeded an interval, probably of anarchy, during which a remnant or offshoot of the invaders struggled with varying fortune against the natives of the country, and at length disappeared from view. The scene again opens with Jye Sheker of Punchásur, his lovely queen, Roop Soonduree, and her gallant and devoted brother, Soor Pál. They belong to the ancient Chowra clan, which had long ruled at Deobunder on the Sauráshtrian coast, not far from the great temple of Somnáth. Driven thence by unexpected

* I take this opportunity of acknowledging my obligations to the works of Tod, Bird, and Briggs, and more especially to the Rás Málá of the late Hon. A. K. Forbes, to consult which is the more necessary, in that original authorities in the vernacular are mostly unprocurable in England, and the more appropriate in that a sketch of events and manners, not a learned addition to local history, is the object at present in view.

enemies, possibly by the fleets of the Arabs, they had retired to Punchásur, on the borders of the Runn, gathered round them the remnants of the power of Vulubhee, and reasserted the national existence of Goozerat. But unfortunately, their praises, sung by a too partial wandering bard, excite the emulation and cupidity of the king of Kuleán in the Deccan, a Rajpoot of the great Solunkhee clan, who has already subdued all other states around him. The defeat of an army sent by him against Jye Sheker only attracts him in person with the flower of his troops, and Punchásur is invested by an overwhelming force. The enemy having gained a footing on the walls after a desperate struggle, Jye Sheker deputes Soor Pál to convey his sister, about shortly to become a mother, to some place of safety, and returns to perish in the breach. Punchásur is taken, Goozerat subdued, and Roop Soonduree compelled to wander in the woods with her infant son. They are at length found by a Jain monk, who recognizes the destiny of the noble child, names him Vun Ráj, or the Forest King, and protects him in his monastery till he can safely join Soor Pál in the fastnesses of Geernár.

The boy accompanied his uncle in many a daring exploit against the Solunkhee conqueror, and from the age of fourteen deliberately set before him the recovery of his father's throne, promising to one of his companions, Chámpá, the post of prime minister; to another, Unhil, the honour of giving his name to a new capital; and to Shree Dévee, a lady who hospitably entertained him, that of anointing him at his installation. But it was not until he had attained the age of fifty and undergone innumerable vicissitudes, that he was able to fulfil these promises to his faithful adherents. In A.D. 746, the Solunkhee expelled, and Goozerat at his feet, he at last laid the foundations of

Unhilwára, destined to be the capital for above six hundred years; Chámpá became his minister, Shree Dévee poured the sacred oil upon his head, while his widowed mother, and the old Jain monk who had preserved them both, witnessed the consummation of their hopes. Vun Ráj died in green old age, leaving his empire consolidated, and his capital attracting, through the ports of the gulfs of Cambay and Kutch, the trade with Africa, Egypt, and Arabia, and embellished with numerous temples and monasteries, of which some of the images, bearing contemporary inscriptions, are still in existence.

His son, Yóg Ráj, combined literary with warlike talents, and joined a confederacy to repel one of the earliest of Mahometan incursions, the first cloud of the gathering storm which was hereafter to burst with unrelenting fury on his native land. During the long reigns of his four immediate successors, Kshem Ráj, Shree Bhoogud, Shree Vair Singh, and Rutnáditya (A.D. 841 to A.D. 935), Goozerat was free from foreign invasion, its sway or influence was extended in various directions beyond its natural borders, and its capital was the centre of an ever-increasing commerce, of which Arabian travellers have left interesting accounts. Sámunt Singh, the successor of Rutnáditya, in an evil hour gave shelter to three brothers, collateral relatives of the ancient national enemy, the Solunkhee of Kuleán, and bestowed on the eldest his sister in marriage. Their son Mool Ráj was handsome and brave, but, as the event proved, selfish and treacherous. Sámunt Singh adopted him, and one day, in half-tipsy fondness, abdicated in his favour. In his sober senses he would have revoked the gift, but Mool Ráj resisted, and murdered his uncle and the rest of his mother's family. Thus, in A.D. 942, the Chowra dynasty was superseded by the Solunkhee, or Chálookya, one of the greatest of the Rajpoot clans, whose progenitor was, as the legend goes, the second to emerge from the mystic fire-fountain of Mount Áboo.

Mool Ráj was scarcely on the throne when he had to withstand a double invasion; on the north from the Chohán chief of Sámbur, or Ajmeer, and on the south from Telingana. Having successfully disposed of both, he commenced several magnificent temples, especially the Roodra Mála, of which remains still exist at Sidhpoor on the banks of the sacred Suruswutee, where Paradise is said to be "only a cubit distant." But war again demanded his attention, and after subduing one unruly feudatory, the chief of Joonagurh, and slaying another, Lákha of Kutch, in single combat, he carried his victorious arms into the heart of the Deccan. "The career of Mool Ráj," says the Rás Málá, "had now reached its limit. Lord of the kingdom of Unhilwára in right of his mother, he had pushed forward its frontier in every direction. Kutch had been subdued by him; the holy land of Soreth obeyed his commands; the inhabitants of the Deccan had beheld his standards flying victoriously beyond the Nerbudda and the range of Injádree; his supremacy was acknowledged by the Purmár prince who ruled in the impregnable towers of Uchulgurh on the summit of the sacred Áboo; and under his leading the chivalrous errants of Marwar and northern India followed, for the first time, the banners of Goojur-Ráshtra. His domestic life had also been prosperous, and he possessed that blessing so invaluable to a Hindoo, and which the most illustrious of the future sovereigns of Unhilpoor were not destined to obtain, a son worthy to be his successor. At the close of his reign, however, Mool Ráj is represented as wandering about painfully from one place of pilgrimage to another, full of remorse for the slaughter of his mother's kindred, and eager only to obtain, at whatever price, the means of expiation." Turning at length to Sidhpoor, he bestowed on the Brahmins, as a propitiatory offering to the deity, Sehore, the old capital of the Sinhas, and Cambay, the chief port of the empire, abdicated in favour of his son Chámoond (A.D. 997), and ended his days in quiet and devotion.

The religious spirit of the later years of Mool Ráj appears to have been brightly reflected on his posterity. His son Chámoond and his grandson Doorlubh both forsook the world for the ascetic life, but some uncertainty exists regarding the duration of their reigns, and whether the latter, or his son Bheem Dev I., was on the throne in A.D. 1024, during the great national calamity of which we are about to speak. If A.D. 1022 be not the correct date of Bheem Dev's accession, as asserted by some, he then commanded his father's armies, and succeeded him about two years later.

While Goozerat had thus been enjoying a long period of repose and good government, the Hindoo kingdoms of the north of India had been facing the ever-advancing storm-wave of Mahometan aggression. In A.D. 977 they had suffered under the great Jeipál a telling defeat, and between A.D. 1001 and A.D. 1022 the Emperor Mahmood of Ghuznee, whose zeal as an iconoclast equalled his success as a warrior, had made a series of devastating inroads, in which the sacred cities of Thánesur and Muttra had been pillaged and destroyed. But one thorn still remained in his side. From the ancient oracle of Someshwur, apparently secure behind its far-off towers overhanging the western waves, "the response still went forth which asserted that the victories of the crescent were but permitted scourges by which an inattentive people was to be compelled to more assiduous worship." Collecting a vast army, Mahmood silently and swiftly crossed the desert from Mooltan, captured Ajmere, skirted Mount Áboo, and surprised Unhilwára. Like the Russian generals of modern days, the Goozerat monarch retired while collecting his forces, and Mahmood passed on to the object of his hate. Somnáth soon lay before him, as it may still be seen, the evening sun pouring its flood of light over time-worn battlement, and snowy surf, and golden sand, and also glancing lightly upon porticos, and spires, and domes which now exist no more. For some days the battle raged fiercely: the army of Unhilwára, under the young Bheem Dev, arrived and fell upon the rear of the invaders, and it was only by great personal valour that Mahmood at a critical moment escaped annihilation and fought his way into the place. Entering the superb shrine of Someshwur, he commenced mutilating the objects of worship, when the priests advanced and offered an enormous sum for their ransom. Mahmood reflected for a moment, and then replied that he was there to break idols, not to sell them, and ordered the work of demolition to proceed. After spending some months in Goozerat he set out to return to Ghuznee, carrying with him as a trophy the sandal-wood gates of the temple. But his retreat was cut off by the unconquerable Bheem Dev, his army was driven into the sandy desert, and he with difficulty reached Mooltan after heavy losses and privations—a lesson apparently long unforgotten, since for a hundred and sixty years the Moslem standards did not again pollute the soil of Goozerat.

Bheem Dev's reign was remarkable for successful foreign wars, and especially for an encounter with Ajmere. After the death of Mahmood, the Hindoo Rajas of northern India combined under the famous Veesul Dev, of that state, and retook many of the districts which had been wrested from them. The pride of Bheem Dev forbade his serving under a foreign prince, so he remained at home, and Veesul Dev invaded Goozerat to punish his neutrality. After a long and bloody engagement the two chiefs agreed that the feud should be forgotten, and a city, called Veesulnuggur, was founded to mark the spot where the Chohán had measured swords with the Solunkhee. The glories of Hindoo architecture which had been veiled for a time by the destruction of Somnáth, were renewed in A.D. 1032 in some of the most exquisite temples in all India, which still grace the hills of Áboo and Arasoor, and in a well, yet existing, built at Unhilwára by Bheem Dev's queen, Oodayámutee. After a reign of fifty years Bheem Dev determined to follow the example of his predecessors, and abdicate in favour of his eldest son. But Kshem Ráj refused to be separated from his father, so, after installing his younger brother Kurun (A.D. 1072), both retired to devote the rest of their lives to the practice of religion.

The peaceful reign of Kurun was an era of national consolidation and great public works, secular as well as religious. A splendid shrine was added to the edifices on Geernár, temples round a tank with stone steps were erected at Modheyra and many other places, and a reservoir, several miles in circumference, called the Kurun Ságur, was constructed, which remained perfect until A.D. 1814, when the neglected embankment was burst by long-continued rain. But another of his works has more interest in connection with this history than any of these. Between the Myhee and Sáburmutee rivers the mountains which form the north-eastern boundary of Goozerat descend to the plain by no sudden transition, but become gently merged in it by innumerable spurs and isolated hills, crossing each other in strange disorder, separated by rapid torrents or blended by thick belts of forest. These again subside into a gently-undulating country, now cultivated sufficiently to resemble the more park-like counties of England and to be cool and salubrious, but in the reign of Kurun still thick with jungle and difficult of access. It was consequently one of the strongholds of the aboriginal tribes to which allusion has already been made, and from it they extended their sway of black-mail and violence far across the rich plain to the westward. Kurun was the first effectually to curb these marauders. Having defeated and slain their chief at Asháwul, he raised a temple to the goddess Kochruv, and built in the vicinity a city called Kurunáwutee, which is frequently mentioned as of importance in his own and succeeding reigns. Through the names of Asháwul and Kochrub, no less than by the extent and importance of the early remains which modern investigations have brought to light, we are able to recognise in Kurunáwutee the city which the Mahometan conqueror, above three hundred years afterwards, converted into his capital under the name of Ahmedabad.

Kurun dying (A.D. 1094) while his son, Sidh Ráj Jye Singh, was a child, the government passed for a time into the hands of the queen-mother, Myenul Dévee, one of those remarkable women of whom the East furnishes examples, even in our own day, who combined the capacity for power with the integrity and will to use it rightly. To public works she was especially partial, and many still in existence are ascribed to her, as, for instance, two vast reservoirs surrounded with stone steps at Veerumgám and Dholka. Her subjects followed her example, and several costly buildings were added to those already erected at Kurunáwutee. Her son resembled her in his tastes, building at Unhilwára a large reservoir surrounded by a thousand shrines, and beautifying Sidhpoor, Geernár, Jhinjoowára, Saila, and various other places with his buildings. Though a good deal under the influence of the Jain doctors, he was liberal in his toleration of all religions, and fond of public theological discussions, some of which took place at Kurunáwutee, also called Shreenuggur, where he occasionally resided. War, however, claimed much of his attention. He carried on a long contest with Málwa, and took its capital after a twelve years' siege, marched an army to the Ganges, and was as extensively obeyed as his great ancestor Mool Ráj had been. Like that prince, he had to subdue his ever-turbulent vassal, the chief of Joonagurh, in Sauráshtra, but under circumstances of melancholy interest. Hearing of a girl in the Joonagurh district, Ránik Dévee by name, who though in humble life, was so lovely that "wherever she moved she left the impress of her feet in rose colour on the ground," Sidh Ráj was betrothed to her, and about to send for her to Unhilwára. Rá Khengár, the chief of Joonagurh and representative of the ancient Yádoo line, heard of this, and thinking it a disgrace that so much beauty should leave his territory, seized Ránik Dévee and married her himself. Sidh Ráj and his army were soon thundering at the gates of Joonagurh. After a long and gallant defence, Rá Khengár died sword in hand on the threshold of his palace, and Ránik Dévee fell into Sidh Ráj's hands. He wished to marry her, but the unfortunate girl passionately entreated permission to follow her lord through the flames, as it was in that age the pride and pleasure of every Rajpootnee to do. Her petition was granted by the chivalrous monarch, and the spot on the banks of the Bhogáwo where she ascended the funeral pile is still marked by the remains of a splendid temple which he erected to her memory.

Sidh Ráj dying in A.D. 1143, without leaving a son, the nobles turned to three brothers, the descendants of Kshem Ráj, who had hitherto lived in obscurity, and placed each in turn upon the throne of Sidh Ráj, that they might decide between them. "The first was quickly rejected," says the Rás Málá, "the effeminacy of his dress exciting general disapprobation. The second prince being seated, was asked by the assembled nobles how he would govern the eighteen regions left by Jye Singh, but his reply,—'according to your counsel and instructions,' sounded tame to the ears of chiefs accustomed to obey the vigorous voice of Sidh Ráj. He was rejected, and Koomár Pál, seated on the throne, was called on to answer the same inquiry. Starting to his feet, his eyes filled with martial fire, that prince half unsheathed his sword. The hall rang with acclamations, and Káhn Dev, with the other nobles of Goozerat, prostrating themselves before the throne of Koomár Pál, while the conch shell and the bugle sounded, acknowledged him as the fit successor of the 'victorious lion.'" Koomár Pál was soon called on to support the character thus acquired in resisting an invasion by the Raja of Ajmere, who sustained a severe defeat, and was glad to escape further punishment by giving a daughter in marriage to the victor. Málwa next felt the weight of his arms, and there are traces of his victories in the Konkun, Meywár, and even the states of the far north. Koomár Pál was as attached to religion and architecture as his predecessors, but greatly under the influence of Hemácháirya, the celebrated Jain monk of Kurunáwutee. The ruined temple at Somnáth received complete restoration at his hands, and new shrines were raised at Táringa, Unhilwára, Dhundooka, Cambay, and many other places. By Hemácharya's advice he endeavoured to stop the destruction of animal life in his dominions, and himself adopted more of the austere life of the Jains than was pleasing to his powerful Brahminical subjects.

Ujye Pál, the nephew of Koomár Pál, succeeded him in A.D. 1174, and commenced a persecution of the Jains, to which his murder put an abrupt termination. His infant son Moolráj was scarcely on the throne when, for the first time since the days of Mahmood, Goozerat was startled by the approach of a Mahometan army. Fortunately, however, Prince Bheem Dev, the uncle of the child, was at hand and scarcely inferior to his illustrious namesake, whose victory he repeated by meeting the army of Shaháboodeen on the frontier, and driving it back with loss into the deserts of Sindh.

In the following year (A.D. 1179), on the death of his nephew, Bheem Dev II. commenced a reign, destined to be the last of the Chálookya dynasty. His gallantry threw a halo over many a well-fought field, while the unfortunate misdirection of his energies contributed not a little to the crushing defeats which resulted in the final ruin of the Hindoo cause. The Ráthor of Kanouj, the Tooár of Delhi, and the Chohán of Ajmere, were at this period the bulwarks of India against the Mahometan powers who were ever pressing on them from Lahore; and had they been able to secure the steady aid of the southern Rajpoot States, the page of Indian history might perhaps have been far different from what it is. But first a daughter of the Purmár of Áboo occasioned a bloody battle between Bheem Dev and the Chohán, and other causes of feud followed in rapid succession. Some cousins of Bheem Dev being at the Chohán court when the praises of their host were being recited by a bard, one of them, fired by the martial lay, unconsciously twisted his moustache, which is a Rajpoot sign of defiance. Supposing an insult intended, one of the Chohán's relatives struck him to the earth. His brother's avenging blades at once gleamed forth, but the strangers were outnumbered and slain.

Again the armies of the Chálookya and the Chohán met, and Bheem Dev avenged his kindred by the defeat and death of Someshwur, the Chief of Ajmere, but in his turn suffered a reverse from Someshwur's son Prithiráj, who united the thrones of Delhi and Ajmere, and is famous in Indian history for his heroism and misfortunes. Turning from Bheem Dev, he gained a victory over Mohummed Ghoree which was the prelude to the final struggle in A.D. 1193, in which the Hindoo confederacy, weakened by fratricidal contests, was broken up, and Prithiráj himself overthrown, taken, and murdered in cold blood. Ajmere, Kanouj, and Benares fell in rapid succession, and Kootub-ud-deen invaded and plundered Goozerat itself in A.D. 1194. Bheem Dev, however, organised a desperate resistance, defeated Kootub-ud-deen in a great battle, and so postponed the establishment of the Mahometan yoke for another century. But the monarchy, though it survived unsubdued, had been shaken to its foundations, and notwithstanding that on the extinction of the Chálookya or Solunkhee race by the death of Bheem Dev II. (A.D. 1215), the sceptre passed to Veer Dhuwul, a chief of the powerful Wághela clan, and was not struck from the hand of his descendants for nearly a hundred years, yet the vigour of united national life had passed away, and the shadow of impending misfortune seemed to hang in dark foreboding over the land.

At this culminating point in the history of Goozerat, a glance may be cast on a few leading characteristics of the political, religious, and social life, as described in the Rás Mála. The State was entitled to a share of the produce of all lands, but this right was in some cases permanently alienated in favour of religious establishments or individuals, and in others delegated to the great feudatories and officers of state. These personages were bound to follow the sovereign with their vassals upon his military expeditions. The conquest of a foreign State implied an obligation thus to act as an auxiliary, and to pay a fixed tribute, rather than the establishment of a new internal administration. "The two prevalent religions, the Jain and the Brahminical, were continually opposed to each other, and gained in turns the mastery," the former being dominant after the time of Sidh Ráj. "Their controversies, though bitter in the extreme, appear to have been conducted with much state and order, and the sovereign, being a Hindoo, sat himself as president of the religious synod." All sects agreed in two points, the necessity of personal piety and self-sacrifice, and the duty of devoting their wealth with unstinting hand to religious purposes, and especially to rearing magnificent edifices in honour of the Deity. These are still to be found in almost every ancient seat, in every stage of preservation or decay; some kept up with jealous care by native millionaires, and annually attracting thousands of pilgrims from all parts of India, others bare upon the lone hill-side or buried in the densest jungle, scarce noticed by the tiger-hunting European, and struggling for existence with creepers which conceal the ruin they silently achieve. Of the capital itself there are numerous accounts from contemporary travellers. "It was to India what Venice was to Europe, the entrepôt of the products of both the eastern and western hemispheres." Temples, colleges, palaces, and squares were, in eastern fashion, interspersed with cooling trees and stately reservoirs, the whole encompassed by walls, many miles in extent, which may yet be traced in the vicinity of the modern Puttun.

"Such, then, are some of the relics of the kings of Unhilwára. Their greatest and most enduring monument is, however, to be found in the fact that, surpassing the boast of Augustus, they found their country a waste, and left it a land flowing with milk and honey." At the time when the Chowra dynasty, under Vun Ráj, first established itself at Unhilwára, large tracts of Goozerat were destitute of other inhabitants than the wild aboriginal tribes. "In the reign of the last of the Solunkhee princes, on the contrary, we behold the same country united under one strong government, studded with wealthy townships, adorned with populous cities, fenced with strong fortresses. The temple lifts its emulous spire above the dark foliage of the grove, out-topped as yet but by the rattling palm; shrine-bordered tanks and galleried wells, right royally devised, are seen in spots moistened of old only by the showers of the monsoon; and strings of camels laden with merchandise, or cavalcades of pilgrims furnished with rich offerings, hardly disturb—so familiar has their appearance now become—the antelope herds which formerly roamed alone over the tenantless plains." In the picture of society which these times present to us, "the prominent figure is undoubtedly the sovereign. He is supported by the white-robed priests of the Jain religion, or by the Brahminical wearers of the badge of regeneration; beside him stand warriors of Rajpoot race in ringed tunics, such as defended from the Saxon bill the knights of the bastard William, or, equally gallant in the field, and wiser far in council, the Wânea Muntreshwurs, already in profession puritans of peace, but not yet drained enough of their fiery Kshutree blood. At the edge of the warlike circle, themselves half warriors, stand the minstrels and the bards, and farther off, fierce only in words, a group of peaceful cultivators, with their offerings of the fruits of the earth, behind whom, trusted perforce, and yet feared, their indispensable guards and yet their plunderers, are ranged the bowmen, the wild aborigines of the ravine and of the hill. The sovereign himself is a stately figure; the scarlet umbrella of royalty is borne above him, the pictured sun glitters in gold behind his head; his necklaces are of voluptuous pearls, and his bracelets are of sparkling diamonds; yet his is no effeminate form; the spear and the brand suit well his massive arms; his eye is red with the fire of battle; the shrill sound of the war shell is as familiar to his ears as the deep rolling of the palatial drum; he is a 'shielded man,' as well as an anointed chief; a 'Kshutree's son,' no less than the offspring of a queen. For the portraits of the fair we must turn to another canvas. There we behold her in the 'swyumbur mundup' choosing her favoured knight, or in the marriage hall shining beside him as the Goddess of Love beside her lord. An honoured mother, we again behold her guiding the realm of her youthful son, or in his manhood aiding him with her counsel, and winning him to works of mercy and religion; or again, alas! we view her in another mood, with strangely frenzied eye, supporting in her lap the lifeless form of her lord, while the shriek of the dissonant horn, and the still harsher scream of superstitious madness afflict the ear, while the funeral flame springs fiercely upwards, and the thick black smoky pall is spread above, as if to hide the horrid sight from heaven."

"The tale of Unhilwára's grandeur has been told; there remains now that of her decay and desolation; yet shall we perceive that her glorious morning shines no less brightly in contrast with the fitful stormy day by which it is succeeded, than first it shone when chasing away the sable clouds of the preceding night," and that the national characteristics which were the basis of her fame gleam forth again and again, at times lending victory to the standards even of the stranger, but oftener renewing with fruitless gallantry the struggle for independence, until at length arises that foreign rule before which Hindoo and Moslem alike sheathe their swords, and gaze with bated breath at the bloodless conquests of order and intellect, directed by the mighty law, "Thou shalt love thy neighbour as thyself."

The reign of Veer Dhuwul, the first of the Wághela dynasty, presents little worthy of note excepting in that it marks the period at which architecture in Goozerat reached its highest developments. Somnáth rose again from its ruins; Shutroonjye received important additions; Chandráwutee, the capital of the Purmárs, who were the great vassals of Unhilwára and lords of Áboo, was embellished; and above all, upon that mount itself, beside the fairy lake, begirt with hills, whose wooded islets float in rich contrast amid the gleams of the setting sun as it seems to plunge beneath its waves, was reared a marble shrine which "for delicacy of carving and minute beauty of detail stands almost unrivalled even in this land of patient and lavish labour." These were among the last great works of the Hindoo dynasties of Goozerat. The time was not far distant when the Moslem conqueror was compelled to bid her enslaved children resort to them for all that was beautiful in plan and detail to lend glory to the edifices of his rival faith, and their influence is, perhaps, not yet exhausted.*

The reigns of Veer Dhuwul's successors, Veesul Dev, Urjoon Dev, Luwun, and Sárung Dev contain little worth notice. Notwith-

* One of the greatest of our Gothic architects recently informed me that he had been glad to borrow details for one of his buildings from the sculptured fragments from Bombay which may be seen in the Museum at South Kensington.

standing internal weakness and growing Mahometan power, the kingdom held together till the reign of Kurun, who ascended the throne in A.D. 1294, and was destined to maintain through a series of years, amidst family bereavement and defection, an heroic but hopeless struggle in successive provinces of his once vast inheritance, and to die at last, uncaptured, unsubdued, but with nothing left except his personal honour and his ancient name.

It has already been mentioned how the gallant Prithiráj, King of Delhi and Ajmere, was overwhelmed and slain, and the Hindoo confederacy of the north finally broken up. Nearly a hundred years were occupied by the Mahometans in consolidating and extending their power to the north and east; during which time Goozerat remained free from molestation. But in A.D. 1297, Alif Khan, the brother of the Sultan Alláh-ud-deen, suddenly appeared with a large force. Kurun was defeated in a great battle, in which his wives, children, and treasure were captured; and the fall of Unhilwára, the sack of Cambay, and the destruction of Sidhpoor and Somnáth followed in rapid succession. The province, however, was not at once subdued. In A.D. 1304 another large army marched against it; and in A.D. 1306, Kurun appears still holding the passes into Khandeish, at the south-eastern corner of Goozerat, and supported by the friendly Raja of Deogurh. His own family here contributed to deepen his misfortunes. His queen, Kowla Dévee, who had been captured in A.D. 1297, had been carried to the imperial harem, and become the favourite sultana of Alláh-ud-deen. She now instigated him to demand the surrender of Dewul Ránee, her daughter by Kurun, who still remained with her father, and was celebrated for her beauty. "The time, however, had not yet arrived when the Rajpoot was accustomed to surrender, in bitterness of heart, his beloved daughter to what he felt to be a pollution worse than death. The clansman of Bheem Dev, the rightful successor of the lion-hearted Sidh Ráj, retained amidst all his misfortunes a sense of the dignity of his race," so the imperial generals prepared to wring the prize from the wounded lion at bay. After a long and fruitless struggle chance threw it into their hands. Dewul Ránee was betrothed to the son of the Raja of Deogurh, and was being conveyed to her future home by a slender escort, when in a defile they met a body of Mahometans who were proceeding to the caves of Ellora. The two parties instantly engaged, and "an arrow piercing the horse of Dewul Ránee, she fell to the ground. A desperate struggle ensued; the swords of Serohee and the scymitars of Arabia, alike reddened with blood, crossed over the prostrate form of the daughter of Kurun; and a misdirected blow might soon have saved the honour of her race at the expense of her life." But it was otherwise ordained. The princess was captured, and conveyed with respect and care to Delhi, where her "incomparable beauty" made her the bride of the heir-apparent. "Yet, while the imperial court rang with the praises of her victorious charms, and the lyre of Umeer Khoosroo immortalised the loves of Khizr Khan and Dewul Ránee, who shall assert that no shade of sadness rested on her spirit at the thought of the disappointed affection of Shunkul Dev, or the deeper grief of her bereaved and dishonoured father?" Her own misfortunes did not end here; for some years afterwards her husband and his whole family were put to death by Khoosroo Khan, a Hindoo renegade whom they had raised to power, and she was transferred to the harem of the usurper.

The history of Goozerat for the next fifty years is that of a series of desperate struggles with the Mahometan governors appointed by the Emperors of Delhi, whose head-quarters were at Unhilwára. To the eastward the centres of resistance were the Ráthors of Edur, and the Gohils of Champaneer, a state founded by the great minister of Vun Ráj; in the centre, towards Sánund, the representatives of Kurun still held much of the country;* and in Sauráshtra the race of Rá Khengár maintained at Joonagurh its ancient love of freedom. At times the Mahometans possessed little more in Goozerat than the encamping-ground of their armies; and even in A.D. 1347, when the Emperor Mohummed Toghluk Shah, at the head of a large army, invaded the country, he sacked Cambay and Surat, but spent two seasons in a fruitless siege of Joonagurh. The campaign produced no lasting results; and the same disorders continued till A.D. 1391, when Moozuffur Khan was appointed viceroy.

Moozuffur Khan was the son of Sehárun, a Rajpoot of the ancient Ták clan, who embraced the Mahometan faith under the name of Wuze-ool-Moolk, and was patronized by the Emperor Feroze Toghluk. Moozuffur, after an unsuccessful attempt to establish himself at Nagore, in Málwa, was made Viceroy of Goozerat, and set himself systematically to the pacification of the country. His most active opponent was the Row of Edur, a state on the north-east frontier, who on three distinct occasions was obliged to yield for a time to the pressure of superior force and pay tribute, but reasserted his independence whenever the Mahometan army was withdrawn. The districts bordering on Khandeish, and those west of Unhilwára, also cost Moozuffur a

* The royal line, whose ancestors thus lost their kingdom about the time when the great monarchies of modern Europe were struggling to establish themselves, still survives in the person of the Chief of Sánund, Queen Victoria's principal tributary in the Ahmedabad district.

campaign, and Somnáth was once more the scene of a victory, followed by the sack of the temples. Fortune shortly, however, bestowed upon him still greater favours. In A.D. 1398 the Moguls, under the famous Tamerlane, swept like an avalanche over northern India, and so permanently disabled the central power at Delhi, that Moozuffur seized the opportunity for assuming independence, and caused himself to be proclaimed Sultan under the title of Moozuffur Shah. Thus was founded the dynasty, which was to maintain in Goozerat for nearly two hundred years a sway, brilliant in its military enterprises and in the architecture with which it adorned its capital; but precarious, ever disputed at lavish cost in blood and treasure, and never effectually established throughout the province.

Moozuffur Shah was succeeded in A.D. 1411 by his grandson, Ahmed Shah, who in the following year determined to transfer the seat of government from Unhilwára to the locality on the banks of the Sáburmuttee, where Kurunáwutee had been founded by the Solunkhee monarch three hundred years before. Modern investigation has not yet proceeded sufficiently far to enable it to be stated with certainty how far Kurunáwutee was contiguous to, or identical with Asháwul and Shreenuggur, both of which names occur in early records as those of a great city hereabouts; but there can be no doubt that the new town of Ahmed Shah, to which he gave the name of AHMEDABAD, and its suburbs, embraced them all, and that his principal edifices are on the desecrated sites of earlier Hindoo buildings, possibly the temples of Kuruneshwur and the monastic retreat of Hemáchárya.

The suggestion of a new capital is ascribed to the king's spiritual adviser, Shekh Ahmed Khuttoo Gunj Buksh, and it was carried out under the personal supervision of "four Ahmeds," viz., Ahmed Shah himself, Shekh Ahmed, Mulik Ahmed, and Kázee Ahmed. An old Hindoo fortification or enclosure, containing a temple of the goddess Bhudra Kálee, was selected as a nucleus; and one of its towers, called Manik Boorooj, is said to contain the foundation-stone. Close by arose a mosque named after the Sultan, a palace which received magnificent additions in subsequent reigns, and other edifices, some of which still survive as public buildings and make the enclosure, yet called "the Bhudder," now, as ever, the seat of government. At a distance of about a mile from the palace, the city walls described a semicircle of some five miles in circumference, resting on the river, and frowning down on it in imposing ramparts fifty feet high or more. The space within the walls was reserved for the Faithful alone; in the suburbs the Hindoo was permitted to locate himself, but the ground in both was partitioned out among the great nobles of the Court, who gradually peopled and adorned their respective quarters, and have bequeathed to them their names. In three years the city was sufficiently advanced for habitation; but the great buildings rose only by degrees; and for upwards of a century the work of population and adornment was carried on with unremitting energy, till architecture could proceed no farther, having satisfied the æsthetic and social wants of above two millions of souls. For materials, the finest edifices of Unhilwára, Chandráwutee, and other cities were ruthlessly plundered; but their delicate sculptures appear, with few exceptions, to have been scornfully thrown into walls and foundations, where they are now constantly found; while for their own works the conquerors resorted to the sandstone quarries of Ahmednuggur and Dhrángadra, or the marble hills of the Ajmere district. As to style, it was the singular fortune of the Mahometans to find themselves among a people their equals in conception, their superiors in execution, and whose tastes had been refined by centuries of cultivation. While moulding them they were moulded by them; and, though insisting on the bold features of their own minaret and pointed arch, they were fain to borrow the pillared hall, the delicate traceries, and rich surface ornaments of their despised and prostrate foe. To describe the varied offspring of this strange union,—to balance the merits and defects of each specimen, and to assign to the whole its proper place in the architecture of India, is the allotted task of a more experienced pen.

The vocation of Ahmed Shah seems, however, to have been to destroy rather than to build, for his whole reign is a series of efforts to break down the liberties, the temples, and the faith of the Hindoo chiefs and landholders of Goozerat, in which he, of course, met with the most determined resistance. Of the latter, or less powerful class, "some sheltered in inaccessible natural fortresses of forest or mountain, were with difficulty compelled to pay a tribute, which was, from the first, always withheld, except when enforced by the presence of superior military power; others, who were less favourably situated for defence, were driven wholly from their lands, and lived the life of outlaws, until their continual harassing incursions drove the proud conqueror to a composition, and they regained, on terms which included submission and tribute, a part of their hereditary domains. Some there were who, urged by persuasion or compelled by force, exchanged the creed of their fathers for Islam, and treated on this account with more consideration, assumed the position of Mahometan zemindars. The work, however, was never fully accomplished; it was a labour of

Sisyphus; allegiance sat as lightly" on the convert as on the Hindoo, and original independence was resumed on every favourable opportunity. Among special causes of irritation were the appointment of an officer commissioned to destroy all temples, and the efforts of Shah Ahmed to replenish his harem. Two stories are characteristic of the spirit with which the latter were received. The Chief of Mátur was invited to Court, and thrown into prison on his refusing to marry his daughter to the sultan. His queen obtained his liberation by surrendering the beauty, named Ráneebá, without his knowledge. On his return she told him what she had done. "The Rajpoot rose, quick as thought, and seized his sword; his wife cast her arms round him, but he dashed her from him to the ground," plunged his sword into his breast, and expired. The gallant Chief of Beola was more fortunate. Feigning consent to a similar demand, he fixed a day for the marriage, but when the sultan arrived at Beola according to invitation, he was attacked by five thousand Rajpoots, and had to carry on a campaign for five months, at the end of which time the Chief escaped with his daughter, and married her to the Row of Edur, the inveterate foe of Ahmed Shah.

With the great princes, such as those of Joonagurh, Champaneer, and Edur, the warfare was more equal and prolonged, and they had a powerful ally in the Sultan of Málwa, who twice penetrated into Goozerat, and whose territories were in turn thrice invaded by Ahmed Shah. Joonagurh and Champaneer were both forced to pay tribute, but Edur, though more than once captured, was never fairly subdued, and, in fact, retained its freedom after the entire dynasty of Ahmed Shah had passed away.

Mohummed Shah succeeded his father in A.D. 1443, and maintained similar struggles with indifferent success till his death, in A.D. 1451. His son, Kootub Shah, preferred foreign to domestic warfare, and combined with the Sultan of Málwa against Koombho Rána, the celebrated poet-king of Meywár, whom they pressed severely, but without making any permanent impression. During the reigns of Kootub Shah and his father, the city of Ahmedabad received fresh embellishment, especially by the splendid mausoleums at Butwa and Sirkhej, and the Kánkria palace and tank.

Mahmood Begurra, the younger brother of Kootub Shah, occupied the throne from A.D. 1459 to 1511, and is the most celebrated of the Mahometan kings of Goozerat. He followed with unswerving energy the oppressive policy of his predecessors in all its forms. Joonagurh first attracted his attention. After two campaigns and a long siege, it was taken, and the Rá was deposed and compelled to embrace the Mahometan faith. Such was the end of the ancient line of princes who had withstood the monarchs of Unhilwára in their palmiest days. Mahmood was now employed for some years in a variety of enterprises by sea as well as land, against foreign and domestic enemies, which it is unnecessary to detail here. The relations of the sultan and the Hindoo landholders may be illustrated by one touching episode. The Chief of Ránpoor, a Gohil Rajpoot, was attacked on some pretence by an overwhelming force. After several actions he was driven back within sight of Ránpoor, and sent word to his wives, that if they saw his royal umbrella go down, they were to destroy themselves to avoid capture. Presently the umbrella bearer thoughtlessly set it down while he drank water. The ladies, who from the battlements watched the fight with straining eyes, at once leaped into the well of the fort and perished. The chief himself was soon afterwards slain on the threshold, and thus spared the pain of entering his desolated home.

In A.D. 1484, Mahmood undertook a more important enterprise, the reduction of the powerful Chief of Champaneer. After a long and bloody siege a breach was at length effected. Then rose from the palace the tall column of smoke which told that the Rajpoots, according to ancient and habitual custom, had committed their wives, their children, and their wealth to the flames, and would soon pour forth to seek death in a final struggle with their enemies. Few survived it except the chief and his minister, who were captured when covered with wounds, and put to death in cold blood on refusing to change their religion. Thus fell the city and state which owed their origin to the great minister of the "Forest King," and had been, with Joonagurh, the chief bulwark of the Hindoo cause. From the reduction of the two the conqueror derived his appellation of Begurra.* Edur alone remained, too weak for extended resistance, yet an incessant thorn in the side of Mahmood and his successors, and a standing encouragement to all minor chieftains.

"Sultan Mahmood, if not the greatest, is certainly the most popular, of the kings of Ahmedabad; he is to the Moslem what Sidh Ráj is to the Hindoo—a nucleus around which gathers romance and tale." His personal strength, courage, and military skill are as conspicuous as his religious bigotry and his stern but farsighted statesmanship. His love for architecture is attested by the cities of Moostufabad and Mahmoodabad, which he founded at Joonagurh and Champaneer, and another Mahmoodabad near Kaira, which contains one of the most beautiful mausoleums in India, as also by the numerous and elaborate

* "Be" means "two," and "gurra" a fort.

additions which his nobles, following his taste, made to Ahmedabad and its environs.

Moozuffur II., the son and successor of Mahmood, was celebrated for his clemency. His reign (A.D. 1511–26) is marked by a six years' war with Edur, and a prolonged but unsuccessful attempt to subdue the famous Rána Sung, king of Meywár. The Portuguese, who had long been ravaging the coasts of Goozerat, and had engaged the fleets of Mahmood Begurra with varied success, captured in A.D. 1515 the ancient Deobunder, the seat of the Chowras, which they still hold under the name of Diu. Damaun fell into their hands in 1558. Bahadoor Shah, the third son of Moozuffur, succeeded him after a brief interregnum, and in a brilliant reign of ten years wrung admissions of his supremacy from the kings of Khandeish, Berar, Ahmednuggur in the Deccan, and Málwa, while he suffered only one reverse, at the hands of the Emperor Hoomayoon. His career was prematurely arrested by death, in an affray arising out of a conference with the Portuguese, upon whom rests the dark suspicion of treachery.

The reign of Bahadoor was, however, but the expiring brilliancy of a setting sun. He and his great predecessors, by their unceasing and fanatic severity, and by their statesmanship in founding Mahometan cities and locating forts and garrisons throughout the country, had for a time trampled down or overawed the Hindoos into submission. But when the succeeding monarchs, Mahmood II. and Ahmed Shah II. (A.D. 1536–61), though personally feeble and in the hands of their followers, attempted to extinguish private rights in the soil, they aroused a resistance more general even than any yet encountered, and more successful, since the rights exist to the present day, while those who threatened them have disappeared from the scene. Hindoo chieftains, great and small, followed the example of the Mahometan nobles in contemning the degenerate central power, till in the time of Moozuffur III., the successor of Ahmed Shah II., the country was practically an infinity of petty states, acknowledging no supremacy except that of superior force.

At this juncture circumstances attracted to Goozerat the attention of the great Akbar, who had been gradually reinvigorating and restoring the enfeebled empire of Delhi. In A.D. 1572 he appeared with overwhelming forces, captured Moozuffer, received the submission of the province, and appointed a lieutenant to govern it in his absence. An insurrection, in which Edur was of course conspicuous, soon recalled him for a time, and in A.D. 1581 Moozuffer escaped, and with the assistance of the Hindoo chiefs carried on for twelve years a struggle for his crown not unworthy of his Rajpoot predecessors. After being at one time in possession of the capital and very extensively acknowledged, he was at length driven from his last retreat in Joonagurh and treacherously betrayed to his enemies, but avoided ill-treatment by committing suicide.

For about one hundred and fifty years subsequent to its invasion by Akbar, Goozerat was governed by the viceroys of the emperors of Delhi, among whom were Shah Jehán and Aurungzebe, before they themselves ascended the Imperial throne. During the first half, at least, of this period, Ahmedabad appears to have been in the zenith of its prosperity. Under Moozuffer Shah III., indeed, almost the last, and not the least beautiful, of the stone mosques had been erected, and subsequent buildings are mostly in the plainer and more massive style of the Patháns; but the viceroys maintained a splendid court, and spared no pains to increase the commerce and general prosperity of the place. It was, in fact, one of the largest capitals of the East, its population above two millions, its suburbs extending for thirty miles round, dignified by sharing with Cabool, Agra, and Bengal alone the privilege of an imperial mint, and enriched by being, like Unhilwára of old, the highway for commerce and travellers between Arabia, Africa, Europe, and all parts of India. Mandelsloe, who visited it in A.D. 1638, observes that "there is scarce any nation in the world, or any commodity in Asia, but may be seen in this city." Its manufactures were gold and silver brocades, silks, satins, velvet, calico, paper, and lackered ware, and its artizans excelled in works in steel, gold, ivory, enamel, and mother-of-pearl. Indigo, cotton, opium, preserves, and spices were the principal exports. The whole country round was "full of gardens and trees;" deer, wild fowl, fish, and the wild boar furnished sport in the vicinity; and he concludes by declaring, "I scarcely know any place in the world where a man may indulge himself with more ease than here." The province generally shared in the prosperity of the capital; and though insurrection was not unfrequent, and each petty state has in this respect a separate and often not inglorious history,* the Hindoo chiefs and landholders found

* Two stories from the Rás Málá may be inserted as characteristic of the times. Veerum Dev, the Row of Edur, happening to pass through Hulwud in Kattiawar, observed that there were no cenotaphs of royal Sutees. The Raja informed him that none of his family had become a Sutee. "What! Has no one of your family married a true Rajpootnee!" exclaimed Veerum Dev, and gave him his sister in marriage, who on her husband's death duly followed him through the flames. On another occasion Veerum Dev, when hard pressed by a Mahometan army, under a prince of the empire, went to his head-quarters accompanied by only one horseman, and asked for an interview, without revealing his rank. He was shown into an upper room, where the prince was seated. While engaged in conversation he noticed a cat that had seized a pigeon drop with it from the roof, and, falling uppermost, escape alive, while the pigeon was killed. Suddenly taking the prince by the throat, he sprang with him in his arms from the window, and killed him by falling on him. He then mounted his horse and escaped, while the army, disconcerted at the loss of its leader, retired from his dominions.

the liberal policy of Akbar a great improvement on the iron despotism of the Ahmedabad kings. Practically, their internal administration was little interfered with, in return for their admitting liability to military service, and to tribute periodically demanded from them by an armed force. Even these restraints became gradually weaker with the progressing enfeeblement of the Delhi empire and the decline of Mahometanism throughout India, till at length a new political status was created by the appearance of other invaders on the scene.

About the beginning of the eighteenth century the Mahrattas of the Deccan, who had long been sapping the foundations of the Imperial government, made their first inroads into Goozerat, their object being plunder rather than conquest. The viceroys were ill able to cope with them; and being deprived alike of aid from Delhi and of the service of their Hindoo feudatories, gradually succumbed, till in A.D. 1755 the Mahometan power in Goozerat was finally extinguished, and the Mahrattas, though divided among themselves, took their place. Excepting around Baroda and Ahmedabad, the nuclei of their power, they had little direct share in the administration of the country, which was left in the hands of the several chiefs; but their armies periodically made the tour of the province to extort an ill-defined tribute, which was never paid except to superior force. It is not necessary here to note in detail either their expeditions or the disputes among themselves, but only that they burnt and plundered the property of friend and foe with almost equal energy, and spared neither mosque nor temple which it suited them to destroy. Innumerable are the architectural monuments which have thus suffered from their wantonness or malice, and the interesting ruins of which the very materials have been carried away for building purposes. Ahmedabad, in particular, felt so heavily the effects of their internal feuds and grinding rule, combined with the natural decay of the Mahometan population, that its suburbs almost disappeared, large quarters within the walls became desolate, many splendid buildings were destroyed, and the remainder were reduced almost to the ruined condition indicated in the photographs of this work. Fortunately, the tide of anarchy was arrested, ere it had wrought even more disastrous results, by the supervention of the British power.

This is not the place to relate how the British first obtained a footing in Goozerat in A.D. 1612, by establishing a factory at Surat; how Surat and Broach afterwards fell into their hands, and their troops took Ahmedabad in A.D. 1780, and Kuree in 1802; how by alliance with one Mahratta state they became mediators between them and the provincial chiefs and landholders, and so put an end to the collection of tribute by devastating armies, and how, by conquering another, they, in 1818, succeeded to its territories and the paramount power. Suffice it to say that since then Ahmedabad and most of the seaboard of the Gulf of Cambay have been British territory; that a tract about equal in extent is held by the Mahratta State of the Guikowar of Baroda, and that the great bulk of the province is in the hands of its original possessors, subject only to the obligation of paying to, or through the hands of the British the trifling tribute to which they may be liable, and of maintaining peace with each other and internal good government. Thus has the mass of the nation acquired, as if in reward for its gallant and prolonged struggles, the greatest measure of freedom to which it ever aspired, coupled with the blessings of a profound peace to which it must otherwise have been ever a stranger, and the example of a civilization which it was incapable of generating from within. On the other hand, the moral of the oppressor is pointed. Whoever visits Goozerat "may behold the subterranean temple of the persecuted Hindoo, and the tall minaret of the Moslem in his day of power and intolerance, and may compare the state of affairs which these recal with things that are. The falling mosque strews the earth with its ruins, while beside it, emerging from their dark hiding-places, the images of Shiva or of Párusnáth are installed in newly-erected temples; and the descendants of the swaggering Patháns and Moguls inlay the marble floors of the Hindoo shrines, or for a pitiful hire wave the torch and beat the drum in those idolatrous processions which gaily move along to re-establish in state the mute gods which their forefathers fancied they had destroyed."

Relieved from the burden which had so long oppressed it, the national life is fast regaining, by channels old and new, its ancient prominence. The "garden of India," fully cultivated by a hardy and intelligent people, sends forth from Dhollera, Broach, and Surat the cotton without which Lancashire would starve; the fierce aborigines are transformed into a vigilant police; the Rajpoot chiefs subscribe capital to traverse with a railway the "holy land of Soreth;" and the Jain and Hindoo merchants direct the money market of Bombay, or the bank and cotton-mill within the very walls of Ahmed Shah. Nor are forgotten the national inclinations towards literature, art, and religion, to account for which by tracing them to the chivalrous and devout character, and the stirring history of the people is the principal object of these pages. The merchant princes lavish their wealth on temples,* which native architects can design as of old, and on hospitals,

* Shutroonjye, especially, receives constant additions. One temple completed there a few years ago cost £170,000. For some of the recent buildings at Ahmedabad, *see* Plates 117 to 120.

colleges, and universities; the chiefs still wear the rich native silks, brocade, and jewellery; and both adorn their houses, outside and in, with the wood-carving which was so much admired at the Great Exhibitions.* Under the liberal patronage of both, too, education is fast spreading through the land; the old national literature is being reproduced; acquaintance with the national architecture is diffused by works such as the present; so that, though the ancient monuments decay the style may live, and expand to suit modern requirements and be the delight of future generations in the Western Presidency, and especially in Ahmedabad, which, now connected by railway with Bombay, and still the capital of Goozerat, is regaining from day to day its old wealth and importance.

* Almost all the black-wood furniture known as "Bombay furniture," and the carved sandal-wood or inlaid work-boxes, &c., called "Bombay boxes," are made either in Goozerat or by Goozeratee workmen and their pupils.

THE CITY OF AHMEDABAD WITH ITS ENVIRONS.

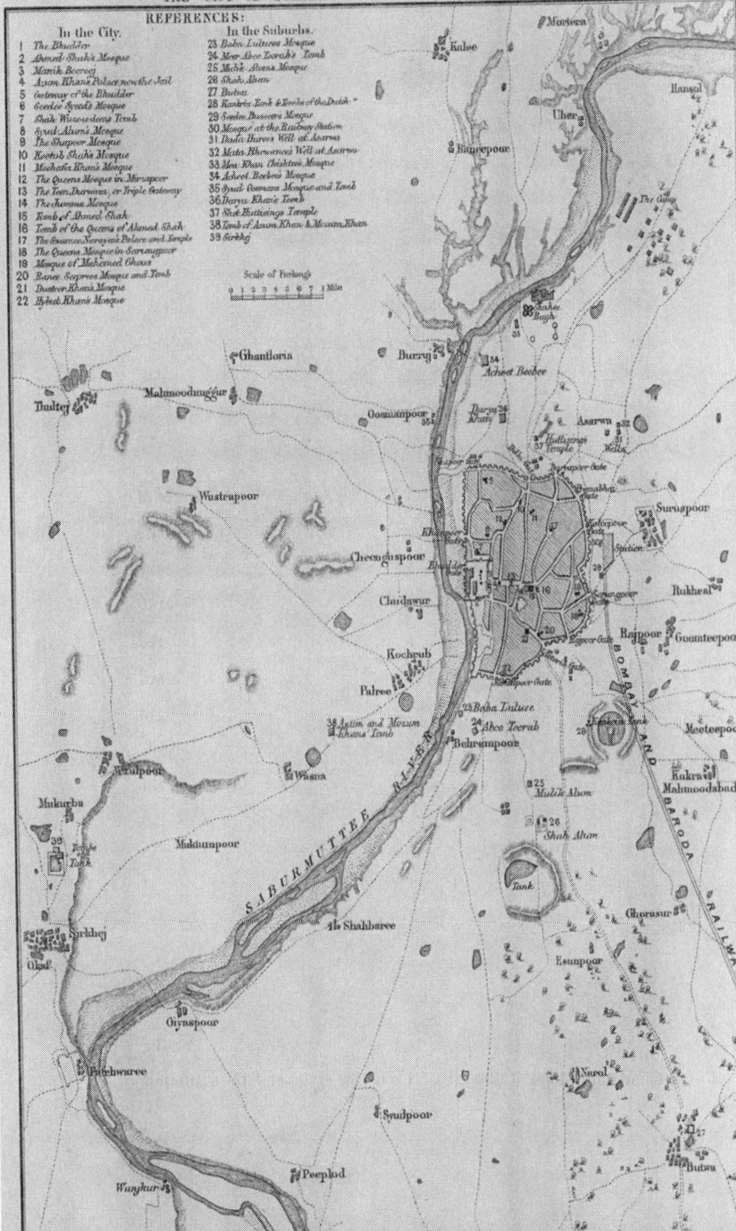

London. John Murray, Albemarle St.

PART II.

DESCRIPTION OF THE BUILDINGS AT AHMEDABAD.

PLATE 1.

Ancient Well of Mátá Bhowánee at Asárwa.

This well is situated in Asárwa, formerly a populous suburb of Ahmedabad, but now more remarkable for beautiful woods. It bears numerous marks of great antiquity, and probably is contemporary with the city of Kurun. As in most of the large wells of Goozerat, the water may be approached by long flights of steps and pillared galleries, the construction of which will be more fully explained hereafter (page 58). The open shafts are here surmounted by light canopies supported by pillars, which may be seen in the photograph, and on the lowest gallery is a small shrine of Mátá Bhowánee, the consort of Shiva, to whom, under attributes resembling those of Isis or Cybele, the well is dedicated.

PLATES 2 and 3.

Ahmed Shah's Mosque.

This mosque is situated in the south-west corner of the ancient enclosure called "the Bhudder," and close to the bastion containing the foundation stone of the city. From its style, and the materials of which it is composed, it appears to have been the first mosque erected by Ahmed Shah, and from its situation within the precincts of the palace, it was ever afterwards the private chapel of the royal household. The façade is undecorated except by a few string-courses and cornices of elementary Hindoo ornament, and is pierced by five large pointed arches and eight windows latticed with perforated stone. The stunted and tapering minarets mark the first efforts of the Hindoo architects to execute these characteristic features of the style of their conquerors. In the interior, five large and several smaller domes, formed of converging stones and richly carved, are supported by rows of pillars mostly taken at random from Hindoo temples, and some of them still bearing (Plate 3) unmutilated figures and emblems. The porch to the north, leading into the latticed "Princesses' Gallery," is unmistakably Hindoo throughout, and may possibly be part of some temple upon whose site the mosque was planted. The pulpit was covered by a canopy, its balustrade is of yellow marble, carved in a leafy pattern, and its steps, as also the whole pavement of the mosque, are white marble. In the courtyard is a mound called "Gunj Sháhid," or the heap of martyrs—the tomb of warriors who perished in fight with the infidel, and were interred here as a special mark of royal favour.

Plates 4 to 6.

Hybut Khan's Mosque.

This mosque is even more illustrative of the earliest attempts to combine Mahometan and Hindoo elements. The plain façade is pierced by three small pointed arches, the minarets, chimney-like in form and dimensions, spring out of the roof, and the centre dome is barely raised above the others by a dwarfed and unlighted clerestory. The columns of the interior (Plate 5), reft from various temples, present every variety of rich ornament, and the parapet of the porch (Plate 6) is essentially Hindoo. Hybut Khan was one of the nobles of Ahmed Shah's court, and built, about the time of the foundation of the city, a suburb which still bears his name. This mosque is said to have been reared in the place of a temple which had been desecrated by slaughtering a cow in it.

Plates 7 to 9.

Syud Alum's Mosque.

This mosque was built by Aboo Bukkur Hooseinee, in the time of Ahmed Shah. Though plain, and evidently early, it shows a considerable advance in power of dealing with the subject.

Plate 10.

Mulik Alum's Mosque.

This mosque was built by Mulik Alum bin Noor Kubeer, styled Wuzeer-ool-Mumálik, in A.D. 1422, and shows additional progress in the new style, and the adaptation of the niche and ornament of the Hindoo spire to the base of the Mahometan minaret. Mulik Alum was a son-in-law of Ahmed Shah, and a clever and brave man, but inclined to rebel, and more than once pardoned on that account.

Plate 11.

The Teen Durwáza, or Triple Gateway.

The ancient enclosure now termed "The Bhudder" has already been mentioned as containing the royal palace and its appendages. The egress from it to the eastward was through a magnificent gateway of three arches, two at right angles to the third, which, though much modernised, may be traced in Plate 114. This gateway led into a large enclosure, forming the outer courtyard of the palace, with a fountain and raised terrace in the centre. Here the great feudatories or foreign embassies assembled before approaching the presence, and the sovereign enthroned on the terrace, mustered the troops for martial enterprises and gala-day reviews, or held splendid Court in the cool of the evening beside the splashing fountain. The enclosure had two side gateways on the north and south, one of which still remains, and a principal one, the subject of the present plate, leading into a broad street traversing the city. Modern buildings have greatly encroached on the space, and a tiled roof surmounts the ruined attic of the Teen Durwáza itself. Through this gateway sallied Mahmood Begurra, at the age of fourteen, to quell by his looks the rebellious nobles who disputed his succession, and in later days, the newly-appointed Mahratta governors used to aim five arrows at one of its beams, and augur good or ill to their administration in accordance with their success in striking it.

PLATES 12 to 20.

The Jumma Mosque.

This splendid edifice, which was completed in A.D. 1423, is situated on the south side of the main street, a little outside the Teen Durwáza, and was originally the centre of a vast square, but has been gradually shut in by the erection of houses against its outer walls. Like all

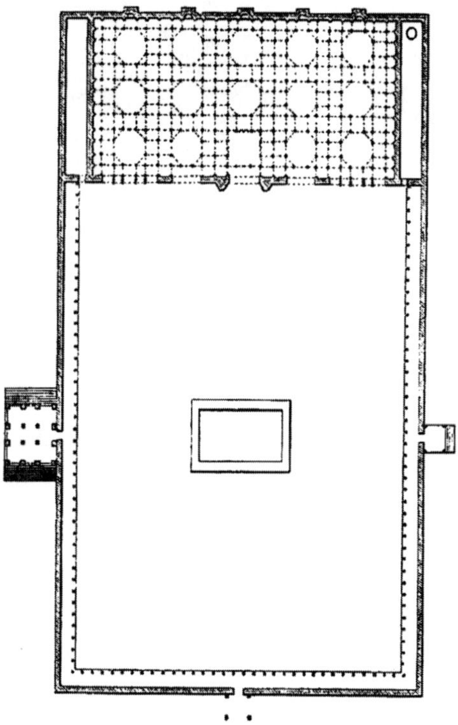

SCALE.—100 feet to 1 inch.

other Mahometan mosques, it faces the east. The plan will be apparent from the annexed woodcut. The northern and southern porches lead into the street, and that to the eastward into an enclosure containing the tomb of Ahmed Shah (Plate 38). In the centre of the courtyard is a reservoir for the ablutions preparatory to prayer. The building is one of the largest in India, the exterior dimensions being 382 feet by 238, and those of the mosque itself 210 by 95, with a height of 49 feet. Further particulars may be derived from the subjoined elevation. The material is the usual fine sandstone, with the

SCALE.—50 feet to 1 inch.

exception of the pavement, which is of white marble. The style shows further proficiency in combining the Hindoo and Mahometan elements and in the use of the native ornament, but few fragments of Hindoo buildings appear to view, excepting the pillars of the clerestory, and perhaps the southern porch (Plate 14), which some have considered to be part of a temple, and *in situ*. The minarets fell, along with most of the others throughout the city, in an earthquake in 1818, but from careful drawings of them which are extant in Forbes's 'Oriental Memoirs,' and Grindlay's 'Scenery, Costumes, and Architecture of Western India,' we learn, that though four-storied, and considerably decorated, they tapered like those of Ahmed Shah's mosque. They and others possessed the peculiarity that when one was shaken the motion was communicated to the other, though no tremor was perceptible in the intervening roof. The interior contains 330 pillars, ranged in magnificent aisles (Plate 18), and supporting, at intervals, domes of converging stones, the interiors and pendents of which are adorned with the most delicate fretwork. The *kiblas*, or points to which all turn in prayer, are inlaid with coloured marbles, disposed in rich harmony of form and colour (Plate 17). On the threshold of the centre arch an inverted Jain image of black marble is embedded in the pavement, to be ever trampled on by the Faithful. The colonnades of the courtyard (Plate 13) are emblazoned with sentences from the Koran.

PLATES 21 to 26.

Ránee Seepree's Mosque and Tomb.

Ránee Seepree was the wife of a son of Ahmed Shah, and her mosque and tomb were completed in A.D. 1431, probably by herself during her lifetime, according to the very general custom. They are the first of a series of buildings more delicately ornate than any which preceded them. The dimensions of the mosque (Plate 25) are 55 feet by 20, and the minarets are 50 feet high. The roof is supported by two rows of six double pillars. The parapet surrounding the tomb (Plate 24) is a rich specimen of Hindoo work, such as has already been noticed in the porches of the mosques of Ahmed Shah and Hybut Khan. Close by is a locality which tradition points out as the ancient Asháwul, where the aboriginal chieftain was defeated by Kurun.

PLATES 27 to 35.

The Queen's Mosque in Mirzapoor.

The exact date of this mosque is uncertain, but in ornament it closely resembles that of Ránee Seepree, and may be assigned to the same period. It derives its name from two royal ladies, whose marble monuments occupy the adjacent tomb (Plate 30), beneath a dome covered internally with fretwork of unusual beauty. One of them reveals her Hindoo origin in her name, Roopáwutee, and was probably one of those unfortunate princesses whom their Rajpoot parents were constrained to surrender in token of submission to the conqueror. The censer and chain is a conspicuous ornament on the monuments and the minarets of the mosque, and the latter show richer and more developed appropriations from the Hindoo spire than heretofore (Plates 32 to 35). The dimensions of the mosque are 105 feet by 46, with a height of 32 feet, and other particulars will be learned from the annexed plan and elevation. The minarets were brought to the ground by the earthquake.

ELEVATION.

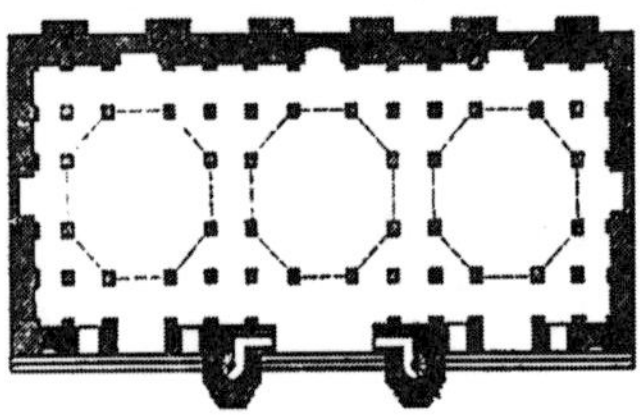

PLAN.

SCALE.—50 feet to 1 inch.

PLATES 36 and 37.

Seedee Syeed's Mosque.

Seedee Syeed was a slave of Ahmed Shah who, like many of his race, rose to wealth and power. He erected within the royal precincts a mosque, which has now been built into the north-eastern corner of the modern wall of "the Bhudder." Its position exposed it in after times to more than usually rough treatment. After being desecrated by the Mahrattas, it has been converted by the British into one of the public offices, and has been hacked about to suit official convenience as much as the Chapter House at Westminster. But its principal glory still remains intact in two windows of perforated marble, which may be safely affirmed to be unrivalled throughout the East. Their dimensions are ten feet wide by seven high.

Plate 38.

Tomb of Ahmed Shah.

The tomb of Ahmed Shah, which is much hidden in the photograph by that of a Mahometan lady and her children, is a massive structure surmounted by a dome, and lighted at intervals by windows of perforated stone. Here repose, with faces turned towards Mecca, the remains of Ahmed Shah, his son Mohummed Shah, and his grandson Kootub Shah, as also of Ahmed Shah II., and others of the family. Their monuments are of white marble, covered with rich silks and besprinkled with rose leaves.

Plates 39 and 40.

Tombs of the Queens of Ahmed Shah I.

Close by the tomb of Ahmed Shah, within an enclosure entered by a lofty gateway, stands, on a basement ten feet above the ground, a noble mausoleum, where, beneath no gloomy darkness of a ponderous dome, but surrounded by the trellised cloister, and now brightening in sunlight radiant as their smiles had been, now overshadowed by foliage graceful as their forms, lie the mouldering beauties of the zenána of Ahmed Shah. The principal tomb (Plate 39), elaborately carved in white marble, and begirt with a

Persian inscription in minute relief, is that of Moglai Beebee. Near it, black marble, inlaid with mother-of-pearl, marks the tomb of Moorkee Beebee, an especial favourite (Plate 40), and others are grouped around.

PLATES 41 to 53.

Sirkhej.

Shekh Ahmed Khuttoo Gunj Buksh was a native of Puttun, as Unhilwára gradually came to be called, and the early friend and adviser of Ahmed Shah. After taking a part in the erection of the new city, as has already been stated, he refused all honour and reward, and retired to Sirkhej, a village about five miles south-west of Ahmedabad, and died there in A.D. 1445. Mohummed Shah, the reigning monarch, ordered a tomb and mosque to be erected to his memory, which were completed in A.D. 1451 by his son Kootub Shah. The locality became a favourite resort of Mahmood Begurra, for repose and religious meditation. He excavated a tank of immense size, surrounded it with steps of cut stone, built on its border a splendid palace and harem, and finally raised a mausoleum for himself and his family opposite to that of the Saint, in which he, his son Moozuffur II., and his queen Rájbaee, are all buried. In A.D. 1584, his descendant, Moozuffur III., suffered a final defeat in the vicinity, which the victorious lieutenant of Akbar commemorated by erecting a pleasure-garden and country-house called Futehwáree, or the "Garden of Victory," of which the remains still exist. The general arrangement of the mosque and tombs will be best understood by reference to the subjoined plan. The palace and harem are at the opposite, or south-west corner of the tank.

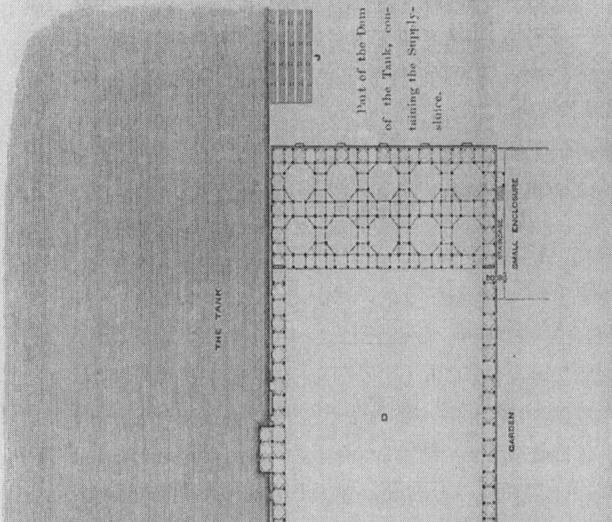

SCALE.—About 100 feet to 1 inch.

REFERENCES :

A. Tomb of Gunj Buksh.—Plate 44.
B. Tomb of Mahmood Begurra and his Sons.
C. Tomb of Beebee Rájbaee, his Queen.
D. The Mosque.—Plate 48.
E. Covered Gateway.—Plate 42.
F. Covered Hall overlooking the Tank.
G. Well and Fountain.
H. Portico leading to Terrace and Steps down to the Tank.—Plate 45.
I. Pavilion.—Plate 43.
J. Portions of the Steps surrounding the Tank.

The tomb of the Saint (Plate 44), which is the largest of its kind in Goozerat, is surrounded by an inner trellis of metal perforated in beautiful patterns, and is dimly lighted by figured perforations in the dome itself. The exterior of both this tomb and the others is entirely filled with windows of perforated stone (Plate 47). The supply-sluice of the tank (Plates 52 and 53) is worthy of notice.

Plate 54.

Kootub Shah's Mosque.

This mosque was built by Kootub-ud-deen in A.D. 1446, during the reign of his father Mohummed Shah. Recently it narrowly escaped mutilation, a proposal having been gravely brought forward in the municipality for cutting off the corner of it in order to straighten the road!

Plates 55 to 57.

Howz-i-Kootub, or Kánkria Tank.

This reservoir is probably the largest of its kind in India, being a regular polygon of thirty-four sides, each side 190 feet long, and therefore considerably more than a mile in circumference. The area is 72 acres. It was entirely surrounded by many tiers of cut stone steps, most of which still remain in tolerable preservation, and had six sloping approaches, flanked by cupolas (Plate 55). The supply-sluice (Plates 56 and 57) is exquisitely carved. In the centre of the tank is an island, connected with the margin by a viaduct of forty-eight arches now in ruins, and which contained a garden called Nugina, and the palace of Ghuttámundul, a favourite resort of the later kings of Ahmedabad. Mandelsloe gives an enthusiastic account of the beauties of the place. It is situated about a mile beyond the city walls, in an undulating and well-wooded country. It was completed by Kootub Shah in A.D. 1451, and is said to have been begun by him in his father's lifetime, in the hope that he might attract, by curiosity, to the works, and there capture and murder his younger brother Mahmood (Begurra), who was living in the neighbourhood with his mother under the protection of the saintly Shah Alum. The name of Kánkria is attributed by some to the limestone found during the excavation, and by others to a pebble (*kánkra*) having got into the shoe and hurt the foot of Mohummed Shah when he came, so runs the tale, to inspect the progress of his son's work.*

Plate 58.

Daryá Khan's Tomb.

This tomb was erected in A.D. 1453, during his lifetime, by Daryá Khan, a talented but abandoned nobleman, who afterwards became a Wuzeer of Mahmood Begurra. It is remarkable for its immense size, the dome being nine feet thick, and the largest in Goozerat. The bad name of its occupant has led to its being thought to be the special habitation of the Powers of Darkness; and on a certain day in the year when the Evil One is supposed to visit it, thousands repair thither at midnight, and come away firmly believing they have seen him.

* These, and other facts and stories, have been obtained from the "Mirát-Ahmadi" and "Mirát Sikunderi," two MS. histories written in Persian in A.D. 1611 and 1756, which are in the India Office Library. Only a portion of the "Mirát Ahmadi" has been translated in Bird's "History of Goozerat."

PLATE 59.

Tomb of Azum Khan and Mozum Khan.

This massive mausoleum, built of brick like that of Daryá Khan, and probably at about the same period, is situated on the road from Ahmedabad to Sirkhej. It contains the remains of two brothers, who came originally from Khorassan, and are popularly believed to have been the architects of Sirkhej. Tradition gives them a bad character. They enriched themselves at the expense of the workmen whom they employed; and it is said that a tank which they constructed never held water, in consequence of the Divine displeasure.

PLATES 60 to 62.

Butwa.

Boorhán-ud-deen Kootub-ool-Alum was descended from the Syuds of Bokhára, and grandson of a famous saint who is buried at Ooch, on

the Sutlej. He was attracted to the court of Ahmed Shah, and settled at Butwa, about six miles from Ahmedabad, where he died in A.D. 1452 in the odour of sanctity. The pious nobles of the court of Kootub Shah and Mahmood Begurra reared over his remains first a small shrine, and then a vast mausoleum (Plate 60), which in proportion and design is equalled only by the contemporary tomb at the city of Mahmoodabad. The aisles are arched and vaulted throughout, and the dome is raised high in air by a second tier of arches. The structure and proportions of the whole will be best understood from the annexed elevation. The outer aisles have now, unfortunately, fallen, and the perforated stonework which must have filled the upper windows, if not also the outer arches below, has entirely disappeared. The monument itself is of most elaborate workmanship, and is

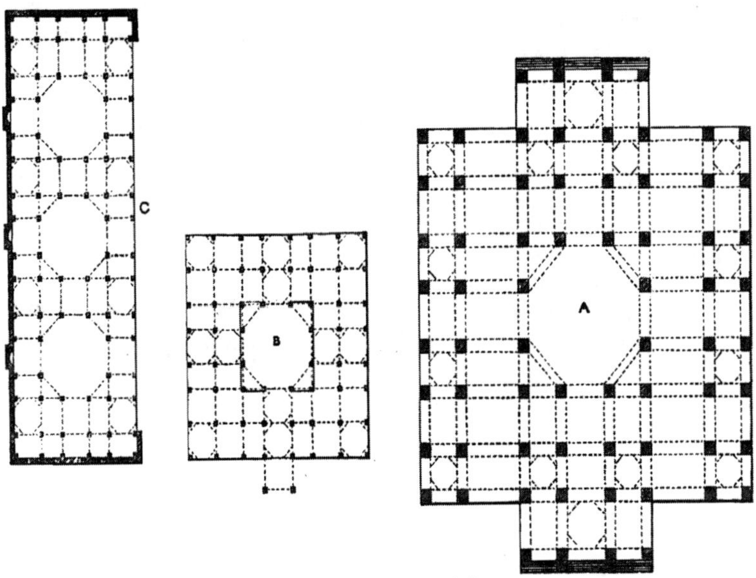

SCALE.—About 50 feet to 1 inch.

REFERENCES:

A. Tomb of Kootub-ool-Alum. B. Tomb of his Son. C. Mosque.

surmounted by a richly-inlaid canopy. A large polygonal tank, a mosque, and a tomb for one of the saint's sons, were subsequently added.

PLATES 63 to 66.

Syud Oosmán's Mosque and Tomb.

Syud Oosmán, called Shumáee Boorhánee, founded a suburb of Ahmedabad, on the west of the Sáburmuttee river, which is still called Oosmánpoor. He died in A.D. 1458, and two years afterward his patron, Mahmood Begurra, built in his memory the tomb and mosque which are here represented. The tomb is 78 feet square, and contains 80 pillars, of which 32 are double. The diameter of the dome is 38 feet. The inner square was enclosed by windows of perforated stone. Oosmánpoor was the scene of some of the contests of Moozuffur Shah III., in the year 1484, for the recovery of his throne.

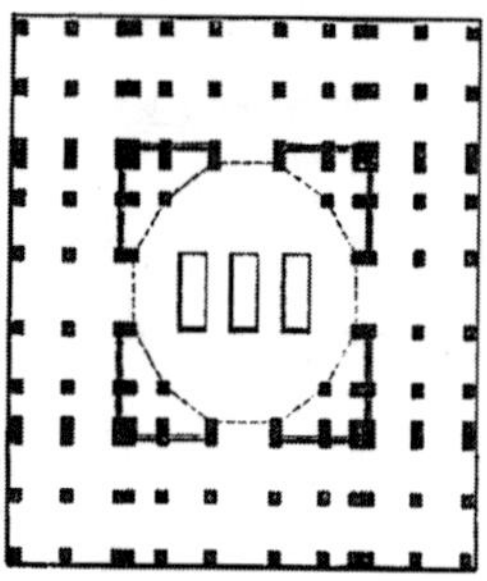

SCALE.—50 feet to 1 inch.

PLATES 67 and 68.

Mea Khan Chishtee's Mosque.

This mosque was built in A.D. 1465 by Mulik Muksood Wuzeer, brother of Mulik Buhá-ud-deen, for Mea Khan Chishtee, and is called after the latter, who was one of a great family which now claims the kazeeship of the city. It is situated about two miles to the north of the city, on an eminence overlooking the Sáburmuttee and close to the royal palace called the Shá̤hi Bágh.

PLATES 69 and 70.

Seedee Busseer's Mosque and Tomb.

The date of these buildings is uncertain, but they closely resemble Mea Khan Chishtee's mosque in many respects, and were erected either by Seedee Busseer, a favourite slave of Sultan Ahmed, whose tomb they contain, or by Mulik Sárung, a noble of the court of Mahmood Begurra, who founded the adjoining quarter of Sarungpoor. They were reduced to ruins in the contest between the Mahrattas and the Mahometan viceroy which took place about A.D. 1755.

PLATES 71 to 81.

Mooháfiz Khan's Mosque.

Jamál-ud-deen, entitled Moohájiz Khan, was a Wuzeer of Mahmood Begurra, who in A.D. 1471 was viceroy of Ahmedabad while

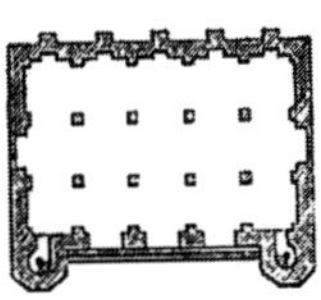

SCALE.—50 feet to 1 inch.

SCALE.—25 feet to 1 inch.

that prince resided at his newly-founded city of Moostufabad, near Geernár. This mosque, which he built in A.D. 1465, is in better preservation than any other in the city, and second to none in beauty. Its dimensions are small, being only 51 feet in length by 36 in breadth, with minarets 55 feet high. The internal arrangement is simple, and the minarets are here, for the first time, placed at the extreme ends of the building. The annexed plan and elevation will afford further explanation.

Plates 82 and 83.

Achoot Beebee's Mosque

Hajee Mulik Buhá-ud-deen, entitled Imád-ool-moolk, or Ikhtiyár-ool-moolk, was a Wuzeer of Mahmood Begurra and the founder of the suburb of Hajeepoor. He erected this mosque in A.D. 1469 for his wife, Beebee Achoot Kookee, whose tomb is close by. The enclosure is unusually large, and was originally adorned with seven minarets, of which three were at the outer, two at the inner entrances, and two on the mosque itself. The earthquake of 1818 completed their ruin. It is situated on the banks of the Sáburmuttee, about a mile from the city, to the northward.

Plates 84 and 85.

The Queen's Mosque in Sárungpoor.

The date of this building is uncertain, but it greatly resembles Achoot Beebee's, and may safely be assigned to the same period.

PLATES 86 and 87.

Dustoor Khan's Mosque.

Dustoor Khan was a Wuzeer in the time of Mahmood Begurra, and his mosque, which is situated close to that of Ránee Seepree, is remarkable for the beauty of the perforated stone screens enclosing a cloister which surrounds the courtyard. The dimensions of the latter are about 75 feet square, and beneath it is a vaulted reservoir of equal size. Such subterranean reservoirs abound throughout Ahmedabad, under mosques, courtyards, and private houses, and some of them, from their size and the beauty of their vaulted aisles, recal the famous Hall of Waters at Constantinople. Occasionally they are provided with a small apartment, with balcony overlooking them, which affords the family a pleasant retreat in the hot season.

PLATE 88.

Ruined Mosque at the Railway Station.

Though these magnificent minarets are the tallest and largest in Ahmedabad, their date, and the very name of the mosque to which they belonged, are lost. Their style and material, however, point to the close of Mahmood Begurra's reign or perhaps rather later. They narrowly escaped removal to make room for the railway, and it is now proposed to incorporate them in a new station built in the Mahometan style. The mosques of Seedee Busseer and Mahomed Ghous, and the walls of the city, appear in the distance in the photograph.

Plate 89.

The City Walls.

The walls of the city, first traced by Ahmed Shah, were placed in thorough order by Mahmood Begurra, in A.D. 1486, and again restored under the British Government in 1832 at a cost of £25,000. They are now in perfect order and fine specimens of such defences, being nearly six miles in circumference, from fifteen to seventy or eighty feet high, and of appropriate thickness. There are numerous towers and bastions, and sixteen gates. The photograph is taken from one of the minarets just described (Plate 88), and shows the surrounding land in process of being laid out for a new commercial suburb called into existence by the railway.

Plates 90 and 91.

Dádá Huree's Well at Asárwa.

Báee Hureer was a lady of the household of Mahmood Begurra, who founded a suburb, called Hureerpoor, within the limits of Asárwa, and built in A.D. 1500 this well, and an adjoining mosque and tomb, in which she is buried. The well has flights of steps and galleries descending to the water, similar in plan to those of the well of Mátá Bhowánee (Plate 1), but far more elaborate, and has no equal in Goozerat, except a well built in the same year by the wife of a Hindoo Chief at the village of Adawluj. Its dimensions at the level of the ground are 196 feet long by 40 wide, and its complicated structure will be best understood from the annexed plan and section. The second shaft of the well is used for irrigational purposes.

The photograph (Plate 90) is taken from the upper gallery, at the well A. The water usually stands at a level of two or three feet below the lower gallery.

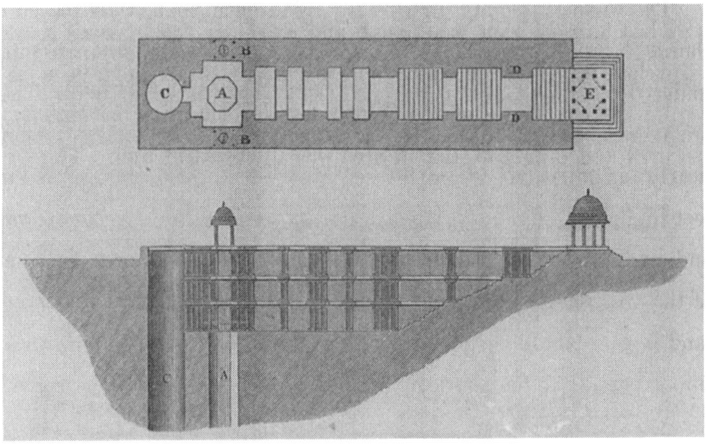

SCALE.—60 feet to 1 inch.

A. Principal Well, octagonal.
B. Spir.l Staircases descending to the Water, surmounted by Cupolas.
C. Well for Irrigation.
D. Inscriptions on the Sides of the Gallery.
E. Domed Porch.

PLATE 92.

Mehráb from a ruined Mosque.

This *mehràb* or *kibla* is a fair specimen of those in the mosques generally, and is loaded with Hindoo ornament. There is usually one *mehráb* opposite each archway of the façade. To the right of the central *mehráb* stands the pulpit.

Plates 93 to 100.

Shah Alum.

Shah Alum was the son of Kootub-ool-Alum, the saint of Butwa who has already been mentioned, and fixed his residence at Rusoolabad, half way between Butwa and the city. He enjoyed in a high degree the confidence of the Court; for the education of Mahmood Begurra and others of the princes was intrusted to him. The con-

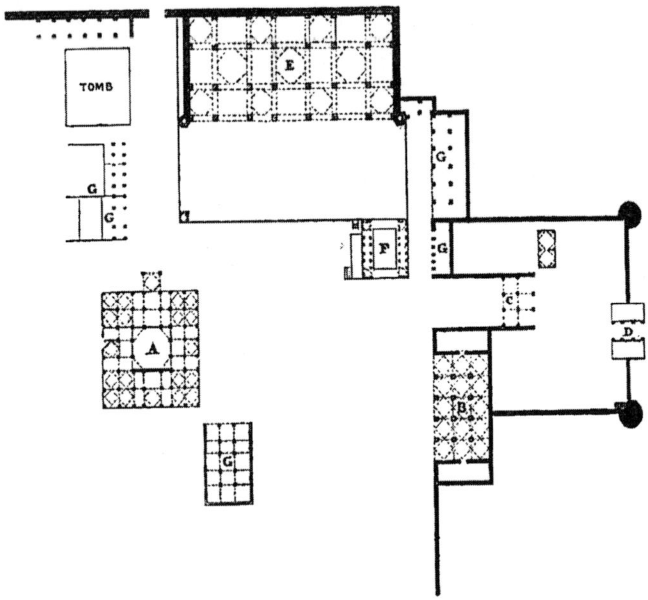

Scale.—About 50 feet to 1 inch.

References:

A. The Tomb of the Saint—Plates 94 and 95.
B. The Assembly Hall—Plate 97.
C. The Inner Gateway—Plate 98.
D. The Outer Gateway—Plate 99.
E. The Mosque—Plates 93 and 100.
F. The Tank of Ablution—Plate 97.
G. Miscellaneous Buildings.

version of the last prince of Joonagurh is attributed to his influence. He died in A.D. 1475, and his tomb was erected by Táj Khan Nariálee, a nobleman of Mahmood's Court. Other buildings clustered round it in subsequent years, and were enclosed by a lofty and bastioned wall, which protected them in troublous times. Their arrangement is shown in the woodcut. According to Briggs, it took ten years to complete the dome. A century afterwards it was gilded and otherwise beautifully ornamented with lapis-lazuli by Asaf Khan, the Wuzeer of the Emperor Jehangeer, and brother of the celebrated Sultana Noor Jehán. The mosque was raised by Mahomed Sálah Badakshi; the minarets were begun by Nijábat Khan, and finished by Saif Khan; and the wife of Táj Khan Nirpoli built the large tank outside the wall, to the westward. The Assembly Hall was added by Moozuffur Shah III., and partly destroyed by the British to furnish materials for the siege in 1780. The group, as a whole, indicates gradual transition of style.

Plates 101 to 103.

Mosque of Mahomed Ghous.

This mosque was built by Shekh Mahomed Ghous Gwaliori in A.D. 1562. It is *sui generis* in Ahmedabad, and more allied to the Mahometan buildings of Beejapoor and Northern India.

Plates 104 to 111.

The Shápoor Mosque.

This mosque was erected by Shekh Hoosein Mohummed Chishtee in A.D. 1565, but the minarets were never finished, owing to the troubles of the time. He died in A.D. 1574. The tracery in the niches of their bases is perhaps superior to any other in the city

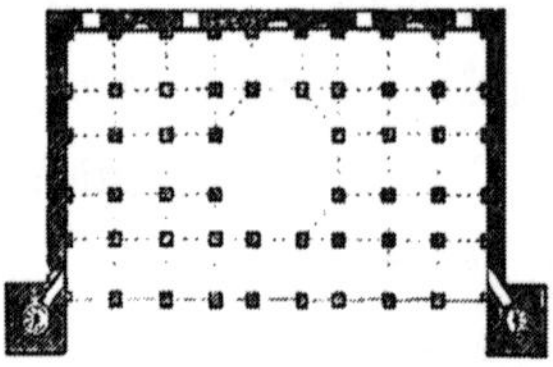

SCALE.—50 feet to 1 inch.

(Plates 106 to 109). The plan is somewhat peculiar, as shown in the margin, and so is the façade (Plate 104). The dimensions are respectable, being 70 feet by 38.

PLATE 112.

Meer Aboo Tooráb's Tomb.

Meer Aboo Tooráb was a nobleman of great talent and influence at the time of the conquest of Goozerat by the Emperor Akbar. He took a leading part in both the pacification of the country under that prince and the troubles consequent on the efforts of Moozuffur Shah III. to regain his throne, for which he was duly rewarded. In A.D. 1579 he was made chief of the yearly caravan proceeding to Mecca, and brought back with him an impression of the prophet's foot, which was forwarded to the emperor at Futtepoor Sikhree in

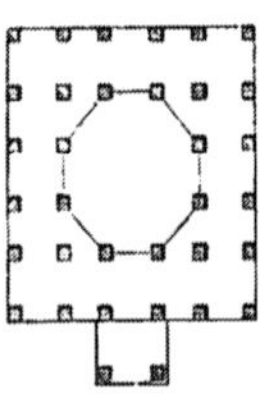

SCALE.—50 ft. to 1 in.

great state. Meer Aboo Tooráb subsequently obtained leave to bring it back to Ahmedabad, and to build there a place for it, of which he was to be the custodian. He did so, and it was for many years a celebrated place of pilgrimage. His tomb is a simple but elegant building, 41 feet square, the inner colonnade of which was enclosed by windows of perforated stone.

Plate 113.

Bábá Luluee's Mosque.

Bábá Mohummed, or Bábá Luluee, as he was called, was a pearl merchant. The exact date of his mosque is unknown, but it resembles the Shápoor mosque, and belongs to this period.

Plate 114.

Azum Khan's Palace.

Azum Khan was an officer of the Imperial Government, whose propensity for building in numerous localities earned for him the nickname of *Oodáee*, or the white ant, which builds its house wherever it goes. He built this palace in A.D. 1636. It was subsequently used as a college, and in 1820 was converted into a jail. The gateway to the right in the photograph is that already alluded to (page 42) as leading into the Bhudder.

Plate 115.

Tombs of the Dutch.

The Dutch had a factory at Ahmedabad early in the seventeenth century, and hospitably entertained Mandelsloe there in A.D. 1638. Their cemetery is on the borders of the Kánkria tank, and contains a number of well-preserved inscriptions, ranging from 1641 to 1699. The building in which they resided still exists in the main street of Ahmedabad.

Plate 116.

Shah Wuze-ud-deen's Tomb.

This was erected in the time of the Emperor Aurungzebe (A.D. 1657—1707), probably towards the close of his reign, and merely marks a period of architectural stagnation.

Plates 117 and 118.

The Swámee Nárâyen's Temple.

Sahajánund Swámee, commonly called Swámee Náráyen, was born near Lucknow in 1780, and at an early age dedicated himself to the reform of the Hindoo faith. His tenets are described by Bishop Heber as a mixture of pure Theism and Hindooism, but he specially inculcated a moral, and even ascetic life. He made numerous converts in Goozerat, and founded there monastic institutions of great magnitude. His successor and representative lives at Ahmedabad, and, under the tolerance of British rule, has within the last few years erected a temple in the old Hindoo style (Plate 117), and an extensive palace or monastery adjoining. The gateway (Plate 118) is still in progress.

Plates 119 and 120.

Shet Huttising's Temple.

The Jain millionaires of the present day have mostly lavished their wealth on temples at Shutroonjye and other sacred seats; but to this there is one great exception in the splendid shrine erected at vast cost by Shet Huttising at Ahmedabad. Its dimensions are of the first order, its style the pure Jaina; and it stands a convincing proof that the native architecture has not been extinguished by centuries of repression, and that in its builder, Premchund Sulát, and his coadjutors, exists a class of practical architects capable, under due encouragement, of taking up and turning to profit the glorious legacy which their ancestors have bequeathed to them.

T. C. H.

PART III.

NOTES ON THE MAHOMEDAN ARCHITECTURE OF AHMEDABAD.

In the beginning of this century the common belief in Europe with regard to India was, that that vast continent was inhabited by one uniform race of Hindoos, steeped in one dreadful superstition, and immutable in their customs and religion from all ages. One by one these delusions have been dispelled. It is now known that the inhabitants of India belong to as many different nationalities as those of Europe; that the number of their sects infinitely exceeds those of any other country in the world; and, so far from being unchangeable, that new sects and new religions are springing up under our eyes, and large populations have adopted new faiths since the rise of our power in that country.

We may, for our present purposes, put on one side the great and manifest distinction which exists between the southern Tamul-speaking races, who came to India in long forgotten pre-historic times, and who still underlie in many corners of the land the Sanscrit-speaking races who crossed the Indus in mythic if not in truly historic times. We may also reject the one hundred and one well-defined varieties into which the various admixtures of these two races have crystallized in the course of time, as our object in this work is to confine our attention wholly to the Mahomedan, and even then we shall find a variety of local forms more than sufficiently numerous, and hardly less perplexing. We know exactly when the followers of the Prophet crossed the Indus. We know also of what race those were who brought the Koran into India. But ethnographically we know little or nothing of the 15,000,000 or 20,000,000 who now profess that religion, and of many who may have done so in the height of the Mogul Empire. Very few indeed were the direct lineal descendants of the original conquerors, and even of these still fewer were untainted with native blood on the mother's side. The bulk were converts in the country, or so mixed up by intermarriages and other local circumstances, as to be hardly distinguishable from the Hindoos except in the form of the faith they professed.

All this is of course expressed in their architecture and their arts, and it consequently requires a vast amount of study before all the forms can be classified and arranged. In Spain, in Egypt, or in Persia, Mahomedan art assumed at once a local form which varied only with the age. In India, on the contrary, the locality must always be also taken into account. If any one fancies that he knows all when he has mastered the details of the art as practised in the imperial cities of Agra and Delhi, he will soon find his mistake. At Juanpore he will find a style as beautiful, but differing in every essential respect. It is no longer the quasi Persian style brought across the Indus, and only slightly modified by local details, but a purely Indian art. The mosques have no minarets, but tall propylons, with sloping sides, like those of Egyptian temples. Their court-yards are surrounded by colonnades such as do not exist elsewhere, and have been mistaken for Buddhist monasteries. At

Gaur an art exists far less pure, and it is only by their plans that we discover that they are dedicated to the simple ritual of the Koran. At Mandoo, another, and far purer style prevails. At Beejapore we seem to have a new importation of pure Toorks established among a people who had no art of their own. But among all these varieties, the most instructive, perhaps, also, it may be added, the most beautiful, is the Moslem style of Goozerat. It bears as strong a local impress as that of Juanpore, while the elements of which it is composed are of even a better and a higher class than are to be found in any part of the Bengal presidency.

The leading events of the history of Goozerat have been so clearly pointed out in the previous chapter that they need hardly be alluded to here, beyond repeating—as bearing on the subject of their art—that from the Christian era to the present time the inhabitants of this country were the most essentially commercial and enterprising of all races of India. In agriculture they were as industrious and as successful as they were valiant in war and patriotic in maintaining their independence. Their architecture, so far as we know it, was always singularly chaste and elegant, and the religion of the dominant class seems to have been essentially Jainism. It is true that the worship of Vishnu and Siva was not unknown in the province, and during a long period Buddhism was established all along its eastern boundary; but the long line of Buddhist caves marks the boundary of the province, and hardly seems ever to have penetrated within its limits. Whether the Jaina religion arose in Goozerat or not, we do not know; but wherever it came from, that province was, during all the time to which our knowledge extends, essentially the home and head-quarters of this faith. Of the Indian forms of religion it is, on the whole, perhaps the purest and the best. It is quite free from the gross and degrading superstition that too generally attaches to the worship of Siva and Vishnu. It is not overlaid by a monstrous priestly asceticism, as Buddhism always seems to have been. It cannot, of course, compare with the vedantic Brahminism which the Aryans brought with them into India; but of indigenous growths, there seems none other so elegant or so pure.

The Mahomedans did all they could, during the time they possessed this province, to stamp it out. On the surface they appeared to be successful; but it survived, and now numbers, probably, as many votaries as it ever did. During the occupation of the province by the Moslems it influenced them and their architecture to an extent they probably would hardly have admitted to themselves, but which makes the charm of this form of art, and gives it a value to the student almost as great as that of any local style we are now acquainted with.

JAINA ARCHITECTURE.

The Mahomedan architecture of Ahmedabad is so essentially derived from the local Jaina forms which it replaced, that, without some knowledge of the former, it is impossible to understand the peculiar merits of that most pleasing variety of the Saracenic architecture of India. It would be as difficult to understand the forms of the Renaissance of Italian art, introduced by Michael Angelo and Palladio, without a knowledge of the Roman art on which it was based. The Corinthian, the Ionic, and Doric orders which these men employed, were not more distinctly of Roman origin than the arrangement of plans and the order of pillars were Jaina which were used by the architects of Goozerat when working under their new masters for a religion they had adopted under extreme pressure from without.

In plan, the great formative idea of Jaina architecture was the octagonal dome resting on horizontal architraves supported by twelve pillars. We have no distinct idea when the form was first introduced into India, no example having yet been found which we can feel certain was erected before the tenth century; but the earliest are as complete and perfect in all their details as any ever constructed afterwards, and therefore were without doubt far from being the first employed. We know also that this form was used occasionally

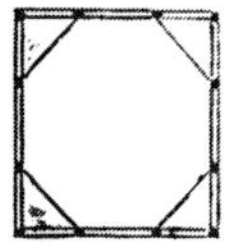

Diagram of the arrangement of the pillars of a Jaina Dome.

Tomb at Mylassa.

by the Romans. At Mylassa, in Caria, there is a tomb erected during the Roman occupation of the country, which is covered by an octagonal dome supported on twelve pillars, and roofed with horizontal layers of stones precisely as the Indian domes are. But we are at once at fault when we come to ask, is this an Indian form imported by some Roman from the East, or is the contrary the case? The derivative forms and the connecting links are both wanting, but from such evidence as is available we may infer that the invention belongs to India; at all events it took no root in the West, while it fructified to an immense extent in the East. The most obvious answer to this view is that the form is not found in the cave temples. This objection, however, will have little weight with those who know how essentially different in nationality and in religious forms the Buddhists were from the Jains, and how different the forms of cave architecture necessarily are from those of structural buildings. Had any of the structural viharas or monasteries of the Buddhists remained to our day, it is not impossible but that this form might have been found in them.

Be this as it may, all the plans of Jaina architecture were elaborated from this one idea. First, two pillars were added on each face, as in Fig. 1. Then four on each face, and two again in front of these, and so till each corner contained fourteen pillars, making fifty-six in all, as in Fig. 2, which is about the extent to which Jaina porches usually extend when used as single features; though they may be, and often are combined together so as to contain hundreds of pillars. Besides the variety of outline and play of light and shade which this arrangement afforded, its great merit lay in the subordination of the parts one to another. Across the centre in both directions was an aisle wider than the others, in the proportion of ten to seven. This, where all the aisles are of the same height, is an infinitely more

Fig. 1.

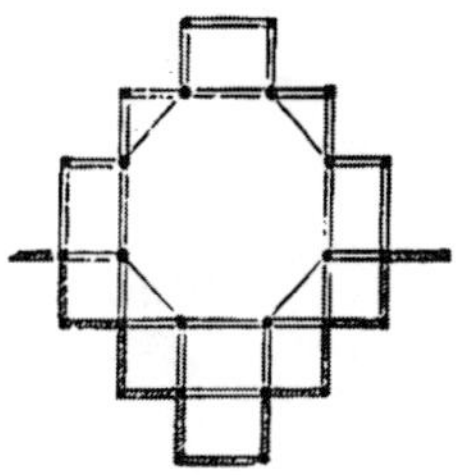

Diagram plan of Jaina Porch.

Fig. 2.

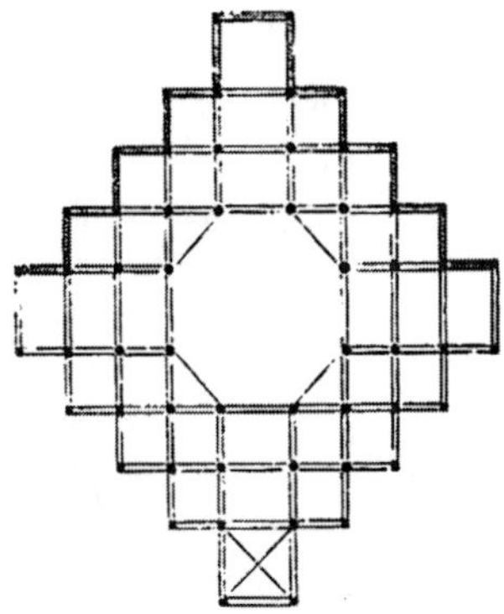

Diagram plan of Jaina Porch.

pleasing ratio than that of two to one, adopted by the Gothic architects, but which was only tolerable where the height was also varied in something like the same proportion. The external appearance of such a porch may be judged of from the view in the next page of a temple near Ajunta. The roof is now ruined, but was composed of a pyramid of steps richly ornamented; and it is doubtful whether the Jains ever allowed the form of their domes to be seen externally. The externally rounded form seems to have been a Mahomedan introduction, copied, shall we say? from the Byzantines.

When the Jains wanted a cell with solid walls, they adopted the same general plan as in their porches, only using double the same number of facets; twenty, for instance, instead of ten, in a first-class example; and enriched each face with sculpture. The great peculiarity of this mode of design is that the entrance, or at least the principal feature, is always on the angle, never on the longer sides, as in all other styles.

Porch of Jain Temple near Ajunta.

The internal appearance of these porches may be judged of from the annexed view of the temple of Veemul Sha, on Mount Aboo. This temple, which was finished in the year 1032, is entirely composed of white marble, and is one of the most perfect specimens of Jaina art to be found in India. The great defect of their porches, in an architectural point of view, is the smallness of their dimensions; and though the elegance and exuberance of their details are such as are admirably suited to their scale, and would be inappropriate to larger buildings, still size is so important an element of architectural effect, that its absence is always to be regretted. In Jaina art it arose from the fundamental fact that no native of India will use an arch except under foreign compulsion. The consequence was that from 10 to

12 feet was as wide a space as could be conveniently used in the wider aisles, and 7 feet to 8 feet 6 inches for the narrower spaces, and

Temple of Veemul Sha, Mount Aboo.

the diameter of the domes was consequently limited to 24 or 30 feet. Even dimensions like these were felt to appear weak in construction, and the Jains in consequence employed an elaborate series of struts under the domes to take off the apparent strain. As now seen they —like the vaulting shafts of the Gothic architects—are merely used to satisfy the eye, rather than the mechanical exigencies of the case.

At the time when Ahmed Shah (1412) undertook to convert Kurunáwutee into the new capital of his dominions, that city no doubt possessed many structures in the Jaina style of architecture, and their destruction afforded not only materials for his new buildings, but hints as to what was most suited to the climate and to the feelings of his subjects; perhaps, it may also be added, to his own, as his blood was Rajpoot, and his wives were the daughters of the Rajpoot nobles of his realm. Unhilwára was then a flourishing city, full of temples and public edifices of every kind. Unfortunately it was situated too near the new capital to be spared, and was used as a quarry during the whole period of the Moslem supremacy. So, too, was Chandráwutee, but it was somewhat more remote; and enough consequently still remains to attest its former greatness and to explain its style. Fortunately, Aboo was too remote and inaccessible to the spoiler; and to it consequently we owe much of the knowledge we possess of the style which the builders of Ahmedabad of necessity adopted.

MAHOMEDAN STYLE.

The problem which the Mahomedan dynasty and its newly-converted adherents set themselves to solve was extremely similar to that presented to the Christians in Italy some ten centuries earlier. In both cases the object was to convert a Pagan style of architecture to the purposes of a religion abominating idolatry. In both, the earlier form of worship was external, the worshippers not being admitted, or only singly, into the sanctuary. Instead of "an ever-present God portrayed in stone," the adoration in both instances came to be addressed to an invisible but omnipresent deity, and by each worshipper from himself assembled in congregation within the precincts of the temple. Perhaps the essential differences between the Jaina and Moslem forms were even greater than between those of Pagan and Christian Rome. The idolatry of the Hindoo was more complete; the adherence of the Moslem to the spirit of the second commandment infinitely more absolute; and the difference greater between a dark idol cell to which no one was admitted, and an open court, whose only purpose was to say, "Mecca is before you!" Though, therefore, the Indian problem may in its conditions have been the more difficult of the two, it was far more satisfactorily solved in so far at least as Ahmedabad was concerned, and in a far shorter time. It was undertaken in 1412, and completed before the death of Ahmed Shah in 1443.

The steps by which this was so rapidly accomplished may easily be traced by any one who will carefully look over and study the first forty photographs of this work, all of which, except the first, represent works erected during his reign; and in the last the Jaina style has already almost disappeared.

The first photograph is devoted to Mátá Bhowánee's Well, one of those works of pious usefulness in which the Hindoos so delighted, and which even the Moslems spared. It is almost the sole vestige of the city of Kurunáwutee, and its architectural details suffice to mark the point to which the style had attained before the city fell. It is more modern than anything at Aboo or Chandráwutee, but older, of course, than anything else now found in the city.

Next comes the Mosque of the Conqueror. Externally its design is imported, and displays all the inaptitude of his recently converted adherents to comprehend what was wanted. The arches, though of the truly pointed type, are so badly constructed as to menace ruin now, and the minarets are hardly more than pinnacles. Internally the Jaina dome is used with considerable success, most of the materials being borrowed from some temple, which must have been pulled down for the purpose and merely fitted together again. On some [see Plate 3] the Hindoo figures still remain.

Hybut Khan's Mosque displays the same peculiarities. An exterior of Moslem severity, designed, probably on purpose, to be as unlike the works of the Hindoos as it is possible to conceive, has internally a Jaina dome of great beauty, resting, as usual, on twelve pillars, two of which are twice the height of the rest, and supported by side aisles also covered with domes, but not rising more than half the height of the central compartment. Its external porch [Plate 6] is the lineal descendant of the Tomb at Mylassa (see woodcut, page 71); and, except the external form of its dome, might have led as appropriately to a temple of the Jain as to a mosque of the Moslem.

In Syud Alum's Mosque a considerable step is made in advance towards harmonizing the external with the internal architecture. The bases of the minarets are of Hindoo architecture, but singularly ill-applied; storey is heaped on storey without apparent motive, balconies are used with no windows opening upon them, and the whole terminates abruptly before amalgamating with the balcony intended to serve as the base of the minaret. The tall pilasters round the side doors are better, but too attenuated, and consequently their form is not found repeated again. The details of the interior are rich as Hindoo art could make them. But the two tall pillars, which are essential parts of the construction of this form of dome, are not happily combined. Apparently the stock of tall pillars, such as those used in Hybut Khan's Mosque, was exhausted; so two small ones were employed, the one standing on the head of the other; and the effect is not quite agreeable. A few years afterwards they would have carved two new pillars for the purpose; but at this stage the supply of old materials seems to have been abundant.

The next example, built in 1422 by Mulik Alum, completes the transition, which had thus only taken eleven years to effect. Here the interior and exterior are brought completely into harmony: the Jaina pillars are no longer concealed behind a mass of masonry of a different style. The design of the minarets commences at the ground, and goes straight through to the summit—a little awkwardly, it must be confessed, but still consistently. The Hindu niches on the base of the minarets have an architectural detail instead of an image, and all parts of the style are settled, wanting only a little more experience to assimilate some parts which have not yet arrived at the harmony they were afterwards destined to attain.

This being so, it may be as well to explain, before going further, one of the most pleasing peculiarities of these mosques; which is, the mode in which light is introduced into the central compartment. So far as is known, it is found only at Ahmedabad, and, consequently, is probably borrowed from some Jaina form of which no examples have yet been found. But whether so, or invented for the nonce, it is one of the most beautiful modes of lighting an interior—especially in a hot climate—ever used; and it is to its introduction that these interiors owe half their claims to our admiration.

The diagram on the next page, used in combination with the plan and elevation of the Mirzapoor Mosque (page 46), will serve to explain this arrangement. The normal type of an Ahmedabad mosque is a building of three squares, each crowned by a dome resting, as usual, on twelve pillars; but the central dome is higher than the other two;

the additional height being obtained by introducing two pillars in front twice the height of the others, and on the other three sides by

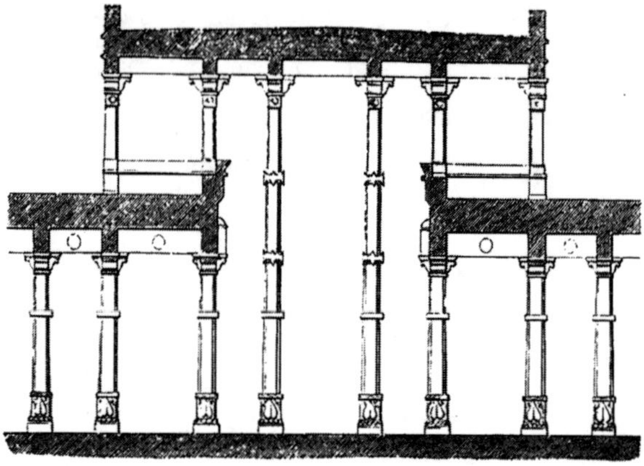

Section of a Mosque at Ahmedabad.

a double range of dwarf columns standing on the roof of the side squares. It will be observed that by this arrangement a subdued reflected light is introduced, without the sun's rays being ever able to penetrate through the attic into the interior; and a most pleasing variety of design is obtained without any undue effort.

This mode of lighting was employed early in the Ahmedabad mosques, and remained so constant and unchanged throughout, that it is impossible to believe that it was invented for the nonce. Like all good things in art, it is evidently the result of long experience, and the residue of many trials. It could hardly, however, have been invented for the purpose to which we here find it applied, because, however beautiful in itself, it affords no protection to the interior of a mosque in the latitude of Ahmedabad before noon. It would have been perfect in Syria, where mosques turn towards the south, but in Goozerat, where Mecca lies nearly due west, the case was different. It would afford the same protection against a northern as against a southern sun, and while leaving the east entirely exposed, it shuts out the rays of the setting sun; all which are anomalies that could hardly have occurred had the mode of lighting been invented for the mosques at Ahmedabad, where alone we now find it.

This mode of lighting has not yet been found in any of the temples of the Jains, though something very like it exists at Sadree, as shown in the annexed woodcut; but this building being lighted

View in the Temple at Sadree.

principally from internal courts, the exact form of this clerestory was not applicable. The probability is that it was used to cover the court-yards of their palaces and dwelling-houses, for which purpose it is in every way perfectly well adapted, and being used more generally for secular purposes, would be all the more readily adapted by the Mahomedans to their mosques.

Returning from this digression, the next building we come to in the series is the Jumma Mosque, the most extensive and splendid of the mosques of the city, and one of the most remarkable of its class in India. Its greater size is not obtained, as it would be in most styles, by any increase in the dimensions of its parts, but by reduplication of the forms already introduced. Thus, instead of three domes north and south, there are five; and instead of only one in depth there are three: making altogether fifteen domes, each with its twelve pillars, but these less than the usual dimensions, being spaced only 6 feet and 8 feet 9 inches apart, instead of 10 feet and 7 feet, as is usually the case. The domes, consequently, are little more than 20 feet wide, except the central range, where a little more extent is obtained by making them oval.

In the great pillared halls of Southern India, where from five hundred to one thousand columns of about these dimensions are spaced equally over the whole floor, the effect is monotonous; and even when a wider central cross aisle divides the phalanx into four, it does not suffice to relieve the mass. The Jain temple at Sadree, shown in plan on the next page, affords a singularly appropriate example of the opposite mode of treatment. It was being erected by Khumbo Rana, of Oodeypore, at the same time as Ahmed Shah was employed in building the mosque, and consequently serves to illustrate the Jaina style as employed simultaneously for its own and for a foreign purpose. The temple is square, enclosing four courts and five shrines. Around these are grouped twenty domes and two hundred and forty pillars, spaced 10 feet and 7 feet apart, and, as shown in the woodcut (page 81), almost identical in design with those of

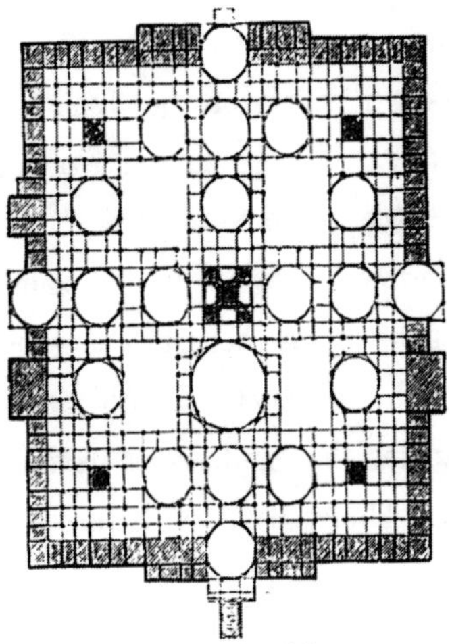

Plan of Temple at Sadree.

SCALE.—100 feet to 1 inch.

the mosque, and the domes also are similar; but though the arrangement at Sadree is highly picturesque, the want of unity is bewildering, and half the effect is lost from absence of simplicity of plan. The plan of the Jumma Mosque is a happy mean between these two extremes. The hall is a simple rectangle, 210 feet by 95 feet; the aisles vary as 10 to 7; and the fifteen domes, arranged symmetrically in three rows, suffice to relieve the monotony of plan without producing confusion, which, with nearly three hundred pillars on a single floor, is a difficulty not easily avoided.

A slight deviation from Jaina detail is observable in the wings, where a bracket imitating a pointed arch is introduced externally, but the effect can hardly be said to be happy.

The northern porch of the mosque is so essentially Hindoo in

M 2

its style that, as Mr. Hope remarks, competent judges have assumed that it is part of a temple *in situ.* The Saracenic arches in its base, which certainly belong to the fifteenth century, quite negative this assumption; and when its details are compared with those of the mosques erected after the date of the Jumma Mosque, it will be seen they are identical. This porch was evidently added after the essential parts of the mosque were complete.

This view is further confirmed by an examination of the next building of the series—Ránee Seepree's Mosque (1431), which is identical in style with the porch, though even more beautiful in detail. Notwithstanding the smallness of its dimensions, it may be considered the gem of Ahmedabad, and, in its class, as one of the most exquisite buildings in the world. It is also one of the most perfectly Hindoo of the buildings of this city, no arch being employed anywhere (except in one side doorway), either constructively or for ornament. The minarets, too, though so exquisite in design, are not minarets in reality; they have no internal stairs, and no galleries from which the call to prayer could be recited. They are pure ornaments, but ot the most graceful kind.

The charm of this building resides in two things. First, the completeness and unity of the design: every form and every detail is designed for the place where it is put, and is appropriate to that place. And next to the fact that all the details are beautiful in themselves, and just sufficient to relieve and accentuate the construction, without ever concealing or interfering with it. It would, of course, be absurd to compare such a building with the Parthenon, or one of our great Gothic cathedrals; but it is, architecturally, a more perfect building than the Erectheion at Athens; and, though we have some Gothic chapels of great beauty, there probably is not one that would not look coarse and plain if placed side by side with this mosque.

The tomb, which stands in front of it, is also very beautiful, but not equal to it in design. The upper storey is too tall for the basement, and not being pierced, while the lower part is, its heaviness is increased to an extent which is certainly unpleasing. This would be less felt if the base were quite free and unencumbered by rubbish, but even then it would have been better if arranged otherwise.

The Queen's Mosque in Mirzapoor belongs to the same age, and its details are as beautiful as those of Ránee Seepree's Mosque, but the design is not so harmonious. It attempts to combine the Mahomedan arcuate style with the Hindoo trabeate architecture; and although the architects had got over much of the awkwardness that characterized their earlier efforts in this direction, they had not yet conquered them. There is, for instance, a very disagreeable contrast between the extreme richness of the minarets on each side of the central arch and the extreme plainness of the arch itself. The richness of the cornice above it adds to the discordant effect. These parts the Hindoo architects could manage perfectly; but how to adorn an arch they did not know, and, strange to say, never learnt. Perhaps it may be said that the building gains in majesty and variety of outline what it loses in unity, by the introduction of these contrasts, and to some extent this is no doubt true. Be this as it may, these two mosques of the Queens may be considered as types of the two forms which the architecture of Ahmedabad took during the period of its prosperity. One, half Mahomedan half Hindoo, combining a pointed arched style with one of pillars and beams only; the other wholly of the latter type, being made up of details and constructive forms invented specially for the arch-hating Hindoos, and merely rearranged to suit the convenience of the new form of worship.

The tomb of the queen who built the Mirzapore Mosque is similar to that of Ranee Sepree; but the architect has seen the defect in proportion pointed out in speaking of that one, and lowered the base of the dome so as to bring it more into harmony with the basement storey of the building.

Perhaps, after all, the greatest beauty of this mosque is to be found in its details, especially in that beautiful form of tracery which fills the niches of the minarets. In every Jaina or Hindoo temple there always is on each face and on each storey a niche which is occupied by a statue or group indicative of the worship to which the temple was dedicated. As the Mahomedans keep the second commandment with the same strictness with which the Scotch observe the fourth, this of course was inadmissible; but as the niche was there, and the Hindoo architects did not know what to substitute in its place, they retained it, but filled it with tracery, sometimes pierced to form a window, sometimes blind, as a mere ornament. Generally these were drawn with so free a hand, and at the same time so gracefully, that they form the most beautiful details, taken singly, to be found in Ahmedabad. All are different, not only in detail but often in character, but all are beautiful. Even these, however, are surpassed by two windows of pointed form found in a desecrated mosque in the Bhudder (Plates 36 and 37). As examples of this class, they are perhaps unrivalled even in India. At Agra and Delhi there are some nearly as fine, but neither so extensive nor so exquisitely balanced as these. There is something wonderfully beautiful in the mode in which construction is, in these examples, combined with mere ornamentation. It is probably more like a work of nature than any other architectural detail that has yet been designed even by the best architects of Greece or of the middle ages.

As every man must do, who wishes a respectable resting-place after death, Ahmed Shah built himself a splendid tomb attached to the great mosque which had been erected during his reign, and beneath its dome he reposes.* The tombs of his queens can hardly be classed as objects of architecture, but they are beautiful specimens of sepulchral art, appropriate to their object, and elegant both in form and detail.

Taken altogether, perhaps the most interesting set of buildings in Ahmedabad and its neighbourhood are those grouped round the Great Tank at Sirkhej. They belong to the best period of the style, 1445 to 1451, and are remarkable throughout for their purity of design and elegance of detail. To the student of Indian architecture, their great interest lies in the fact that they are almost wholly Hindoo, or more correctly Jaina, in their style, with only the slightest possible reminiscence of what might be called Saracenic architecture in any part. The only arches to be seen are the three of the entrance gateway (Plate 42), and one great constructive arch in the Palace (Plate 51). There are arched forms in the tomb of the Saint (Plate 44), but they are only brackets. All the rest are as completely Jaina as are the temples on Mount Aboo or that at Sadree.

The mosque (Plate 48) is only slightly less in dimensions than the Jumma Mosque, and, like it, is five domes in width, but the pillars

* The little tomb with two domes in the foreground of Plate 38 must not be mistaken for that of the monarch. It is of very much more modern date. The building in the back ground is the Tomb of Ahmed.

are fewer in number, more widely spaced, and more elegantly arranged. It may be questioned whether the absence of the arched frontispiece is not to be regretted; but on the whole, considering what a mosque really is, and how difficult it is to amalgamate these two somewhat incongruous parts, it is somewhat difficult to decide which is most beautiful. It is clear that the architects of that day were quite unable to make up their minds on this point, one half of the mosques of Ahmedabad being of the one type, the other half as persistently of the other. It is quite evident, however, that at the time when this mosque was completed, the favourite architect at court understood far better the design of a columnar than of an arcuate building, for the mosque of Kootub-ud-deen (Plate 54) is certainly the least successful attempt that was made at Ahmedabad in this direction; and we cannot consequently but feel glad that the same style was not employed at Sirkhej.

We in Europe are proud of the walls of glass that enclose the naves of our cathedrals. Are they more beautiful than the wall of trellis-work which encloses the Tomb of the Saint (Plates 43 & 44)? Considering the enormous variety of design involved in such a screen as this, the beauty of the patterns, and the effect of the subdued light which they shed internally, there is something in all this which it would not be easy to match in any part of the world.

The palace of the Alhambra at Granada was erected about a century earlier than this; and, if this were the place to do it, few things would be more interesting than to institute a comparison between them. In the eastern palace personal luxury is almost entirely subordinated to religious aspirations. In the western palace religion is hid away in a corner. The Turanian blood of the eastern monarchs shows itself everywhere in the loving contemplation of death and its symbols which everywhere prevails; while nothing suggestive of the tomb is to be found in the western monarch's palace. But the most striking contrast is in points of detail and elegance of constructive propriety which characterize every part of the palace at Sirkhej, and which are wholly wanting in the staring plaster decorations of the Alhambra. Yet we have hundreds of volumes illustrating the glories of Granada, but this is the first to introduce to the public in Europe the beauties of Ahmedabad.

The next group in the series, that at Butwa, advances the investigation one step further in the development of the style. We have a mosque and tomb in the same style as those at Sirkhej, but we have also a tomb—that of Kootub-ool-Alum—in which the arch supplies the place of the beam, and gives, in consequence, immensely increased dimensions to the building, and it must be admitted with very considerable beauty and propriety of effect; but here the arch is used consistently throughout—it is not a screen of arches hiding a columnar interior, but one design uniform in all its parts. A Hindoo, however, would point in triumph to the ruined state of the arcades of the larger building, while the pillars of his thrustless construction still stand erect and undisturbed.*

At Oosmanpoor we again revert to our Hindoo style. Arches being strictly prohibited, the mosque itself is in the style of that of Ránee Seepree (Plates 21 and 26), or that of Sirkhej (Plate 48), but

* In justice, however, to the designer of the arched tomb, it ought to be stated that at Mahmoodabad, near Kaira, there is a tomb in the same style, of the same age, and possibly designed by the same architect; but being less influenced by Hindoo principles than in the capital, he so arranged his building as to be perfectly stable to this day, though quite as extensive as this one. (A view of it was published by Capt. Grindlay in his Views in Western India.)

with the advantage over the latter of possessing minarets, the want of which is the great defect of that group; but the arrangement of the pillars is neither so simple nor so clearly expressive of the internal arrangement of the domes as at Sirkhej. The tomb, too, introduces us to a novelty, being supported directly on twelve pillars instead of eight. In the principal tomb at Sirkhej (see woodcut, p. 49) something of the sort was attempted, but the dome there was octagonal, and the area square, so that there is a want of constructive harmony, which is obviated in this instance. The first was an experiment, and in it, the defect being seen, the remedy was suggested and applied at Oosmanpoor. As originally erected, its effect must have been considerably enhanced by a screen wall which enclosed the central square. The outer ranges of columns then formed a double verandah around the sanctuary, but this screen has now disappeared.

The mosque of Mooháfiz Khan (1465) is the exact counterpart in dimensions of the mosque of Ránee Seepree, and affords a curious means of comparing the columnar with the arched style, but wholly in favour of the former. The earlier mosque is one of the most beautiful in Ahmedabad; that of Mooháfiz undoubtedly the least so, either externally or internally, of all those erected during the great age in that city. Its form and arrangements are very unpleasing, but its defects in design are to some extent redeemed by the beauty of its details. The base of its minarets, the sculptured tracery of its niches, the richness of its galleries, and the careful execution of the whole, spread a charm over its ugliness which it is difficult to resist. Elsewhere these might compel us to admire; here they must be put on one side; and we cannot help being surprised that such a design should be perpetrated in such a place and age.

We now come to a series of mosques all in the mixed style,—those of Mea Khan Chishtee, 1465, of Seedee Busseer, Achoot Beebee, 1469, and the Queen's Mosque in Sarungpoor—which bring the mosque-building history of Ahmedabad down to the death of Mahmood Begurra, 1511, exactly one hundred years after the accession of Ahmed. We have thus, in the space of one hundred years, a style of architecture attempted, experimented upon, and finally perfected, either in its normal condition as a Hindoo style, or as mixed with Mahomedan details, but these so perfectly amalgamated—as in the case of the mosque of Achoot Beebee—that it requires a practised eye to detect what belongs to the one style, what to the other. Taken altogether the result perhaps presents as beautiful a composition as ever was made of materials at first sight so discordant.

After this period we have only one example of any importance in this style, in the Shápoor Mosque (A.D. 1565), and if we consider it as two separate designs, it is very beautiful. The centre part is a very happy attempt to combine the beauties and appropriateness, for mosque purposes, of the pillared style with a certain amount of arcuation. It is simple and chaste, and when complete must have been of great elegance. The minarets, also, so far as executed, are equal to anything in the city. Some of the details, especially the tracery of the niches, surpass almost any others; but the two parts are only placed in juxtaposition, without any attempt to fuse them together, and so far from aiding, they injure each other by the contrast they challenge between the unadorned simplicity of the centre as compared with the exuberant richness of the wings.

The mosque of Bábá Luluee is of the same age and style as the last, but from the discrepancy between the centre and wings not being so great, it is, on the whole, perhaps, a more pleasing specimen; but, on the other hand, its central dome wants sufficient dignity for its situation.

The tomb of Aboo Tooráb exhibits the peculiar phases of the art in its most pleasing form. It is still the style of Ahmedabad, though the columns have entirely passed away, to give place to the arch which here pervades every part. This tomb, however, is a more pleasing example of it than the two mosques last quoted, because it is of one uniform style throughout. No minarets in *quasi* Hindoo style contrast with its plainness and disturb the harmony of the design, while the three larger and two smaller arches on each face announce the existence of the octagon dome, and relieve the monotony of the sides without becoming elements of confusion.

The remaining Mosques of Ahmedabad.—Those of Shah Alum and Mahomed Ghous are more of the usual form of Mahomedan buildings in other parts of India, and can scarcely be said to belong to the local style described above. The latter, especially, looks like a bad transcription of the Juanpore mosques, and though not deficient in a certain amount of grandeur, is painfully wanting in elegance. The tombs of Shah Alum (1475), still retain their local character to a great extent, and are still pleasing; so, indeed, are the buildings grouped around them. These, however, are such as may be found in any city between Lahore and Hyderabad, full of picturesqueness of outline and poetry of design, but deficient in grandeur and that peculiar local charm which is so attractive in the smaller buildings of Ahmedabad. The interiors, however, of both these mosques (Plates 100 and 103) are well worthy of study by those who have not had an opportunity of becoming acquainted with the grander examples of this form of construction at Agra and Delhi. The mode in which the pendentives are brought up to receive the circular dome is quite as happy as any of the constructive expedients of the Gothic architects, and more elegant in execution. The Byzantine architects never accomplished this—their peculiar expedient—so successfully.

After the destruction of the national independence by Akbar (1572), the monuments of every class became fewer and less pleasing than those of the earlier epoch; but the spirit of art was inherent in the people, and whenever it had an opportunity it still cropped out, but more in their tombs and smaller buildings than in their mosques or palaces. The tomb of Shah Wuze-ud-deen (Plate 116), though erected probably as late as 1700, is still a very beautiful monument, or at least would be thought so in any other city than this. The principal dome may be too tall, and the want of a central point in the longer front unpleasing, but its traceried windows are still elegant, and the whole composition by no means wanting in grace.

In the above notes on the architecture of Ahmedabad, two tombs have been passed over. Those of Darya Khan (1457), and of Azum Khan, of about the same date (Plates 58 and 59). They are both built in brick, and belong to a style as different from that above described as Gothic is from Roman. There are hundreds, perhaps it would be safe to say thousands, of such tombs scattered over the plains of Hindostan. They are solid, massive buildings, unmistakably appropriate to the purpose to which they are dedicated, and capable of an expression of sublimity—as we shall see at Beejapore—to which the more elegant style of Ahmedabad could not attain. If gloom is to be associated with the grave, this is the more appropriate style of the two; but this was not the manner in which death presented itself to the sovereigns of Ahmedabad in the great age, and the cheerful elegance with which they surrounded their burying-places shadowed forth a happier philosophy.

Whatever credit we may be inclined to award to those who invented the Jaina style of architecture, or to those who carried it to such a degree of perfection in the old times of Hindoo rule, still we cannot doubt, but that in passing through the ordeal of the Mahomedan conquest, it was very much purified, and many new combinations introduced of great ingenuity and beauty. Notwithstanding all their efforts to stamp it out, the Jaina faith continued to be practised, and buildings to be erected for its purposes, during the whole period of the Mahomedan Empire; and when the volume of photographs of Jaina architecture comes to be published, the public will be in a position to judge how far the style was altered or improved by the Mahomedans. Meanwhile there are two modern buildings illustrated in this volume which show the style as it now is. One, the temple of Huttising (Plates 119 and 120), is finished, and comparing its details with those of Aboo, or those of Chandráwutee, as shown in the woodcut on the opposite page, we see at a glance that the style is the same in its general features, but having lost much of its purity though nothing of its richness. The other, a Hindoo temple of Swámee Náráyen (Plates 117 and 118), was hardly finished when the photographs were taken. Its gateway is still incomplete, and is open to the same criticism—lace-like in detail, but wanting in purity and in perfection of proportion; but still so beautiful, that it would be extremely interesting if the materials existed to trace back its form to the original.

As it happens, however, the architecture of the province of Goozerat is so essentially Jaina, that it is extremely difficult to see what the

Pillars at Chandráwutee, belonging to a ruined Jaina temple erected in the 13th century.

style of the worshippers of Siva or Vishnu may have been in former days. At present it differs in no essential respect from that of the followers of the Jaina Teerthunkers. In the Temple of Swámee Nárâyen the three spires which cover the cells where the images are placed are identical with those used by the Jaina architects, and the porch is very nearly so. Its principal feature is an octagonal dome supported on twelve pillars, as explained above (page 72), causing the pillars to be spaced in the ratio of 10 to 7. The one difference that can be detected is that the angles are filled in, making the porch squarer than is usual in Jaina temples, though this form may sometimes be used by them also; but whether or not, it certainly is not an improvement, and destroys that play of outline which is the great charm of the original arrangement. Barring this slight defect, the design of the whole is not unworthy of the great days of the earlier style.

The temple which Shet Huttising completed about twenty years ago, is dedicated to Dhurmanáth, one of the twenty-four deified mortals whom the Jains reverence as rulers of the world. Two of their number, Adeenáth, who was the first, and Nemeenáth, the twenty-second, are said to have died in Goozerat, and to them most of the temples in that province are dedicated. The plan of the temple follows the time-honoured arrangements which were adopted at Mount Aboo at least as early as the beginning of the eleventh century, and have been followed with very little variation to the present day. The principal feature in all these temples is the "Vimána"—square at the base, and containing a cell in which the principal image of the saint is placed. Sometimes there are three such, as in this instance; at other times—as at Sadree (see woodcut, page 83)—four cells containing images are placed back to back. These cells are always surmounted by a "Sikra" or spire, of that peculiar form shown in the engraving on the opposite page, and which, with the Jains, seem hardly to have varied during the last eight centuries. In front of this sanctuary there are always one or more porches. In this instance the principal one is two stories in height, and in front of this again is an open porch surmounted by a dome, supported on twelve columns, arranged as explained above.

VIEW OF THE TEMPLE OF SHET HUTTISING AT AHMEDABAD.

These features form the temple proper; but in this example, as at Aboo, at Sadree, and, indeed, wherever the temple is complete, the whole is enclosed by a range of smaller cells, each containing an image of the same saint to whom the temple is dedicated, or in some instances one is appropriated to each of the twenty-four Teerthunkers, as they are called. At Aboo every cell is ornamented with bas-reliefs in white marble, illustrating passages in the life of the saint, and in modern times at least these are generally surmounted by Sikras or spires of the usual form. As will be seen from the woodcut, this gives a dignity to the outer enclosure, combined with a meaning which is seldom found in any other style of architecture, and the whole arrangement leads pleasingly up to the principal feature, showing great skill in the subordination of the various parts. In the centre of the principal front of this enclosure facing the temple is an external gateway, the features of which are illustrated in Plates 119 and 120.

It will startle many to be told that even buildings so original as these are being erected in sight of the Doric pillars of the verandah of the Collector's Bungalow and the sham Gothic of the Padre's Church. It is not only in Goozerat, however, but wherever native feelings are allowed to prevail, that buildings as beautiful as these, some more so, are daily springing up, and with very slight encouragement might be made far more numerous and beautiful than they are. Not only does the Hindoo still love art, but he still instinctively adheres to the only system by which good architecture was ever yet produced in any part of the world. It is the system which enabled our forefathers to build those wonderful churches which still excite our admiration and our envy, and which we foolishly fancy we can reproduce by copying. The Hindoo knows better, and can consequently do better things; his system is right, though unfortunately his standard is not so high as his well-wishers would desire.

1. ANCIENT WELL OF MÁTA BHOWÁNEE AT ASÁRWA.

2. AHMED SHAH'S MOSQUE.

3. AHMED SHAH'S MOSQUE.—*Hindoo Pillars.*

4, HYBUT KHAN'S MOSQUE.

5. HYBUT KHAN'S MOSQUE.—*Hindoo Pillars.*

6. HYBUT KHAN'S MOSQUE.—*The Porch.*

7. SYUD ALUM'S MOSQUE.

8. SYUD ALUM'S MOSQUE.—*From the South.*

9. SYUD ALUM'S MOSQUE.—*The centre Arch.*

D

10. MULIK ALUM'S MOSQUE.

11. THE TEEN DURWÁZA, OR TRIPLE GATEWAY.

12. THE JUMMA MOSQUE.

13. THE JUMMA MOSQUE.—*Part of the Northern Colonnade.*

14. THE JUMMA MOSQUE.—*Hindoo Porch in the centre of the Southern Colonnade.*

15. THE JUMMA MOSQUE.—*Nearer view.*

16. THE JUMMA MOSQUE.—*The centre Arch.*

17. THE JUMMA MOSQUE.—*The central Mehrâb.*

F

18. THE JUMMA MOSQUE.—*Pillars in the Interior.*

F 2

19. THE JUMMA MOSQUE.—*Niche between the central and side Arch.*

20. THE JUMMA MOSQUE.—*Niche between the side Arches.*

21. RÁNEE SEEPREE'S MOSQUE AND TOMB.

22. RÁNEE SEEPREE.—*Southern end of the Mosque.*

23. RÁNEE SEEPREE.—*The Tomb, from the North-east.*

24. RÁNEE SEEPREE.—*Base of the Tomb.*

25. RÁNEE SEEPREE.—*The Mosque.*

H

26. RÁNEE SEEPREE.—*Northern corner of the Mosque.*

H 2

27. THE QUEEN'S MOSQUE IN MIRZAPOOR.

28. THE QUEEN'S MOSQUE IN MIRZAPOOR.—*The Interior.*

29. THE QUEEN'S MOSQUE IN MIRZAPOOR.—*Base of the Northern Minaret.*

I

30. THE QUEEN'S MOSQUE IN MIRZAPOOR.—*The adjacent Tomb.*

31. THE QUEEN'S MOSQUE IN MIRZAPOOR.—*The Northern Side-arch and Windows.*

32. THE QUEEN'S MOSQUE IN MIRZAPOOR.—*Niche in lower part of base of Northern Minaret.*

35. THE QUEEN'S MOSQUE IN MIRZAPOOR.—*Niches in upper part of base of Southern Minaret.*

33. THE QUEEN'S MOSQUE IN MIRZAPOOR.—*Niches in upper part of base of Northern Minaret.*

K

34. THE QUEEN'S MOSQUE IN MIRZAPOOR.—*Niche in lower part of base of Southern Minaret.*

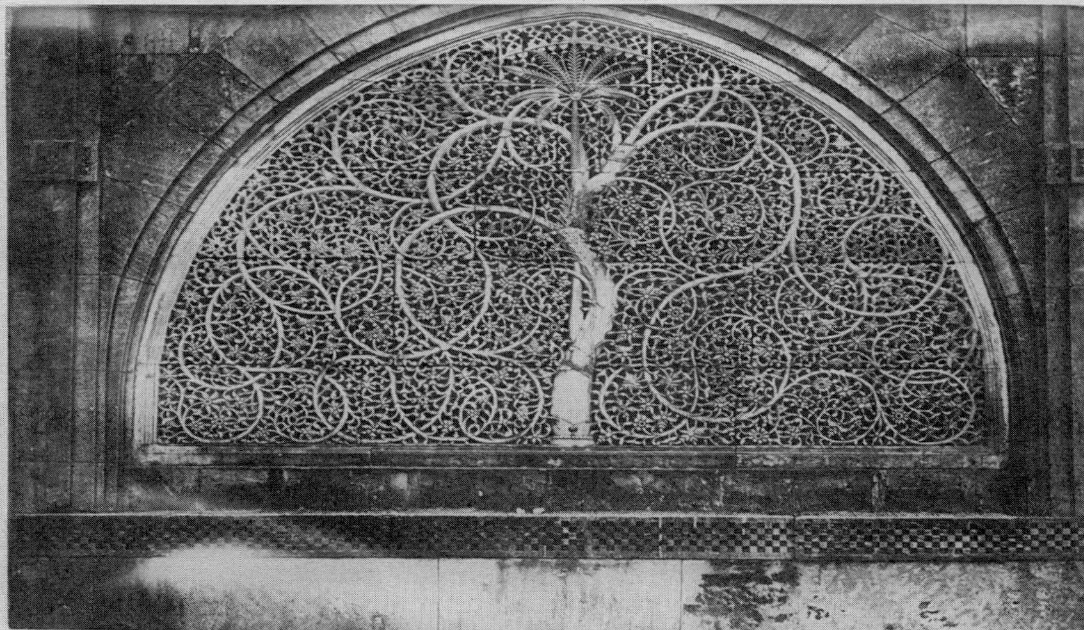

36. SEEDEE SYEED'S MOSQUE.—*Window of perforated Marble.*

37. SEEDEE SYEED'S MOSQUE.—*Window of perforated Marble.*

L

38. TOMB OF AHMED SHAH I.

39. TOMB OF THE QUEENS OF AHMED SHAH I.

40. TOMB OF THE QUEENS OF AHMED SHAH I.

41. SIRKHEJ.—*View from the South-west corner of the Tank.*

M

42. SIRKHEJ.—*The entrance.*

43. SIRKHEJ.—*The Pavilion, and the Tomb of Gunj Baksh.*

44. SIRKHEJ.—*The Tomb of Gunj Buksh, from the North-east.*

45. SIRKHEJ.—*Porch between the Tombs of Mahmood Begurra and his Queen.*

46. SIRKHEJ.—*View from the South-east.*

N 2

47. SIRKHEJ.—*The South-west corner of the Tomb of Mahmood Begurra.*

48. SIRKHEJ.—*The Mosque, from the North-east.*

49. SIRKHEJ.—*Porch in the Southern Colonnade of the Mosque.*

50. SIRKHEJ.—*Ruins of the Harem of the Palace.*

51. SIRKHEJ.—*The Waste-weir of the Tank, and part of the Palace.*

52. SIRKHEJ.—*The Supply-sluice of the Tank.*

53. SIRKHEJ.—*The Supply-sluice, and the Palace in the distance.*

54. KOOTUB SHAH'S MOSQUE.

55. HOWZ-I-KOOTUB, OR KÁNKRIA TANK.—*Cupola at one of the approaches.*

56. HOWZ-I-KOOTUB, OR KÁNKRIA TANK.—*The Supply-sluice.*

57. HOWZ-I-KOOTUB, OR KÁNKRIA TANK.—*The Strainer of the Supply-sluice.*

58. DARYÁ KHAN'S TOMB.

59. TOMB OF AZUM KHAN AND MOZUM KHAN.

60. BUTWA.—*The Tomb of Kootub-i-Alum.*

61. BUTWA.—*Tombs of Kootub-i-Alum and his Son.*

62. BUTWA.—*The Tombs and Mosque.*

63. SYUD OOSMÁN'S MOSQUE AND TOMB.—*From the North-east.*

64 SYUD OOSMÁN'S MOSQUE.

65. SYUD OOSMÁN'S TOMB.—*Part of the North side.*

66. SYUD OOSMÁN'S TOMB.—*The Interior.*

67. MEA KHAN CHISHTEE'S MOSQUE.

68. MEA KHAN CHISHTEE'S MOSQUE.—*Near View.*

69. SEEDEE BUSSEER'S MOSQUE AND TOMB.

T

70. SEEDEE BUSSEER'S MOSQUE.—*Near View.*

71. MOOHÁFIZ KHAN'S MOSQUE.

72. MOOHÁFIZ KHAN'S MOSQUE.—*Near View.*

73. MOOHÁFIZ KHAN'S MOSQUE.—*Northern Minaret.*

U

74. MOOHÁFIZ KHAN'S MOSQUE.—*Niche in lower part of base of Northern Minaret.*

75. MOOHÁFIZ KHAN'S MOSQUE.—*Niches in centre of base of Northern Minaret.*

76. MOOHÁFIZ KHAN'S MOSQUE.—*Summit of a Minaret.*

77. MOOHÁFIZ KHAN'S MOSQUE.—*Base of Southern Minaret.*

x

79. MOOHÁFIZ KHAN'S MOSQUE.—*Niche in lower part of base of Southern Minaret.*

78. MOOHÁFIZ KHAN'S MOSQUE.—*Niches at base of Southern Minaret.*

X 2

80. MOOHÁFIZ KHÁN'S MOSQUE.—*Niches in centre of base of Southern Minaret.*

81. MOOHÁFIZ KHAN'S MOSQUE.—*Niche in base of Minaret.*

Y

82. ACHOOT BEEBEE'S MOSQUE.

63. ACHOOT BEEBEE'S MOSQUE.—*The adjacent Tomb.*

84. THE QUEEN'S MOSQUE IN SÁRUNGPOOR.

85. THE QUEEN'S MOSQUE.—*Central Arch.*

86. DUSTOOR KHAN'S MOSQUE.—*The Colonnade.*

87. DUSTOOR KHAN'S MOSQUE.—*Perforated stone Windows.*

88. RUINED MOSQUE AT THE RAILWAY STATION.

89. THE CITY WALLS.

30. DÁDÁ HUREE'S WELL AT ASÁRWA.—*The upper Gallery.*

91. DÁDÁ HUREE'S WELL AT ASÁRWA.—*Cupolas over the Staircases.*

92. A MEHRAB FROM A RUINED MOSQUE.

93. SHAH ALUM.—*The Mosque.*

94. SHAH ALUM.—*The Tomb of the Saint.*

95. SHAH ALUM.—*The Saint's Tomb, from the West.*

96. SHAH ALUM.—*A small Tomb.*

97. SHAH ALUM.—*The Tank, Assembly Hall, and Entrance.*

98. SHAH ALUM.—*The inner Gateway.*

99. SHAH ALUM.—*The outer Gateway.*

100. SHAH ALUM.—*Interior of the Mosque.*

101. MOSQUE OF MAHOMED GHOUS.

102. MOSQUE OF MAHOMED GHOUS.—*From the North.*

2 D 2

103. MOSQUE OF MAHOMED GHOUS.—*The Interior.*

104. THE SHÁPOOR MOSQUE.

105. THE SHÁPOOR MOSQUE.—*Base of the Northern Minaret.*

2 E

106. THE SHÁPOOR MOSQUE.—*Niches from the base of the Northern Minaret.*

107. THE SHÁPOOR MOSQUE.—*Niche from the base of the Northern Minaret.*

108. THE SHÁPOOR MOSQUE.—*Niches from the base of the Southern Minaret.*

109. THE SHÁPOOR MOSQUE.—*Niche from the base of the Southern Minaret.*

2 F

110. THE SHÁPOOR MOSQUE.—*Window of perforated stone.*

111. THE SHĀPOOR MOSQUE.—*Window of perforated stone.*

112. MEER ABOO TOORÁB'S TOMB.

113. BÁBÁ LULUEE'S MOSQUE.

114. AZUM KHAN'S PALACE, NOW USED AS THE JAIL.

115. TOMBS OF THE DUTCH.

116. SHAH WUZE-U-DEEN'S TOMB.

117. THE SWAMEE NÁRÁYEN'S TEMPLE.

2 H 2

NÁRÁYEN'S PALACE

119. SHET HUTTISING'S TEMPLE.—*The Porch.*

120. SHET HUTTISING'S TEMPLE.—*The Entrance.*